Managing your Academic Career

Universities into the 21st Century

Series Editors: Noel Entwistle and Roger King

Further titles are in preparation

Managing your Academic Career

Wyn Grant with Philippa Sherrington

First published 2006 by
PALGRAVE MACMILLAN
Houndmills, Basingstoke, Hampshire RG21 6XS and
175 Fifth Avenue, New York, N.Y. 10010
Companies and representatives throughout the world

PALGRAVE MACMILLAN is the global academic imprint of the Palgrave
Macmillan division of St. Martin's Press, LLC and of Palgrave Macmillan Ltd.
Macmillan® is a registered trademark in the United States, United Kingdom
and other countries. Palgrave is a registered trademark in the European
Union and other countries.

ISBN-13: 978–1–4039–4548–8
ISBN-10: 1–4039–4548–9

This book is printed on paper suitable for recycling and made from fully
managed and sustained forest sources.

A catalogue record for this book is available from the British Library.

10   9   8   7   6   5   4   3   2   1
15   14   13   12   11   10   09   08   07   06

Printed and bound in China

Contents

Tables

Boxes

Series Editors' Preface

The series is designed to fill a niche between publications about universities and colleges that focus exclusively on the practical concerns of university teachers, managers or policy makers and those which are written with an academic, research-based audience in mind that provide detailed evidence, argument and conclusions. The books in this series are intended to build upon evidence and conceptual frameworks in discussing issues that are of direct interest to those concerned with universities. The issues in the series will cover a broad range, from the activities of teachers and students, to wider developments in policy, at local, national and international levels.

The current pressures on academic and administrative staff, and university managers, mean that only rarely can they justify the time needed to read lengthy descriptions of research findings. The aim, therefore, is to produce compact, readable books that in many parts provide a synthesis and overview of often seemingly disparate issues.

Some of the books, such as the first in the series *The University in the Global Age*, are deliberately broad in focus and conceptualization, looking at the system as a whole in an international perspective, and are a collection of integrated chapters, written by specialist authors. In other books, such as *Research and Teaching: Beyond the Divide*, the author looks within universities at a specific issue to examine what constitutes 'best practice' through a lens of available theory and research evidence.

Underpinning arguments where appropriate with research-based conceptual analysis makes the books more convincing to an academic audience, while the link to 'good practice and policy' avoids the remoteness that comes from an over-abstract approach. The series will thus appeal not just to those working within higher education, but also to a wider audience interested in knowing more about an organization that is attracting increasing government and media attention.

NOEL ENTWISTLE
ROGER KING

Preface

This book had its origins in suggestions made by younger colleagues in the Department of Politics and International Studies at Warwick University. They had observed that while I had enjoyed a reasonably successful academic career, I did not seem to work excessively long hours and found plenty of time for my leisure interests. They thought I might have some 'secret' that I could share. I do not have any secret formula, no potion that can be ingested or mantra that can be chanted, although my early training as a journalist taught me how to produce crisp prose to very tight deadlines. It did seem to me that there might be scope for a book that provided systematic advice for recent entrants to an academic career on how they might manage their career to achieve their own particular goals. One book fulfilling this purpose was available in the UK (published in the late 1990s) and there were a number of American titles.

Two decisions were made at an early stage of planning the book. Higher education systems still differ substantially in a number of respects from one country to another and it is not yet possible to write a book that covers a number of different systems. This book is therefore written for a UK audience, although it may well have some value for academics in other systems. Second, the experience of being an academic is significantly different in a number of ways in the natural sciences, not least because of the importance of laboratory work. This book may have some relevance for natural scientists, but it is directed primarily at academics in the humanities and social sciences.

I invited Philippa Sherrington, who had won an award for teaching excellence at Warwick, to assist me in writing the book. Philippa wrote the chapter on teaching, but has read all the other chapters and contributed to their content. Philippa also brought the perspective of a younger person at an earlier stage of her career to the writing of the book.

I am conscious of the fact that I am at a very different stage of my career from the individuals at whom this book is aimed. I was appointed at Warwick in 1971, a product of the 1944 Education Act. I was the first person in my family ever to attend university. I entered an academic environment that was much less pressured, complex and challenging than it is today, although it was also an environment in which little systematic support was offered to new entrants. The extent and complexity of the challenges facing new entrants to an academic career is one reason for writing this book, although it is also important to emphasize that contemporary academic life also offers new opportunities and mechanisms of career advancement.

There is a tension between offering structured guidance in a book of this kind and being didactic or patronizing. Some of the mistakes made by new entrants identified in this book might seem obvious and easily avoidable, but everyday experience does suggest that similar mistakes are made time and time again. This book does not tell readers what their goals should be, although work in the humanities and social sciences should seek to advance our understanding of the human condition and enable students to develop a capacity for independent thought and critical judgement. The book does not seek to substitute the values of the authors for those of readers, but it does point to the strategies and tactics that can be used by new entrants to achieve the goals they have set for themselves. It does not seek to offer a pathway to career success, not that there is any one such pathway anyway, but it does provide guidance on how to deal with the common problems encountered by new researchers and teachers.

In order to understand the challenges and hopes of young academics, the two authors conducted semi-structured interviews with university lecturers at early stages of their careers in a range of disciplines in the humanities and social sciences and at different types of universities. Thirteen semi-structured interviews of about one hour's duration were conducted in 2004 and 2005, seven with respondents in the humanities and six with respondents in the social sciences, six respondents coming from post-1992 universities. The interviews were usually conducted in their offices and were recorded. Those interviewed were in no sense a proper sample or a large one, but their comments and observations were of immense value in informing the writing of this book. A number of quotations from them, referred to by fictitious first names, appear throughout the book and help to bring the challenges faced by young academics to life. I am very grateful to them for agreeing to be interviewed.

Dr Nicola Phillips of the University of Manchester (formerly at Warwick) was one of the people who inspired me to write this book. She found time from her busy schedule to read through each chapter draft as it was written and I am very grateful to her for her sagacious comments, which have greatly improved the book. I am also very grateful to my research assistant, Justin Greaves, who read the manuscript from the perspective of someone at the start of his academic career and made many valuable comments that helped me to improve the manuscript. Rosalind Martin read parts of the book from the point of view of someone who is a contemporary of those written about, but has pursued a career more typical of her generation, that of a successful entrepreneur. None of these individuals is responsible for any deficiencies in the book.

Suzannah Burywood was a model editor of the book at Palgrave Macmillan. It was good to make contact again with the series editor, Roger King, whom I first knew as a fellow academic in my own field, but who went on to a successful career in academic management, eventually as a vice-chancellor. Alan Curbishley has been, as he has for many years, an inspiration in terms of his people skills and the ways he copes with the pressures of being a Premiership football manager, which he has discussed with me on many occasions. Any academics who think they face competing pressures on their time and have to deal with difficult individuals should spend some time with a Premiership football manager.

I was the first academic in my family and I will probably be the last. None of our children have chosen an academic career. Whether my grandchildren (Clarissa, Lauren and Victoria) will choose such a career remains to be seen. It is a career that in some ways has become less attractive than it once was, but it remains the right choice for a particular type of person: someone who is excited by ideas and their communication to others. It is hard work and the financial rewards do not compare with those in many other professions, particularly given the time it takes to secure a permanent post, but there are many other satisfactions that it offers. Even research universities may, however, find it difficult to recruit and retain staff of a sufficiently high quality in the long term as higher education in the UK faces many difficult challenges. The introduction of substantial fees at undergraduate level will increase the financial pressures faced by graduate students during the long period of apprenticeship. It is not unusual for someone to get a first permanent full time job in his or her early thirties and the level of compensation received is not sufficient to easily wipe out the debts that have accumulated.

Finally, my thanks go to my wife Maggie, my companion for over 30 years. Coming from a similar background in south-east London and pursuing a career in further education, she has shared with me the rewards that a career in teaching and writing can bring, as well as a love of cats and football.

WYN GRANT

Abbreviations

AERC	Alcohol Education and Research Council
AHRC	Arts and Humanities Research Council (formerly Arts and Humanities Research Board (AHRB))
ALCS	Authors' Licensing and Copyright Society
AUT	Association of University Teachers
COST	European Cooperation in the field of Scientific and Technical Research
Defra	Department of the Environment, Food and Rural Affairs
DFID	Department for International Development
EPSRC	Engineering and Physical Sciences Research Council
ESRC	Economic and Social Research Council
FDI	foreign direct investment
FEC	full economic costing
FP	framework programmes
HEFCE	Higher Education Funding Council for England
HEI	higher education institute
JRF	Joseph Rowntree Foundation
NATFHE	National Association of Teachers in Further and Higher Education
OST	Office of Science and Technology
PDF	post-doctoral fellowship
PLR	public lending right
QAA	Quality Assurance Agency
RAE	research assessment exercises
RELU	Rural Economy and Land Use programme
UCU	Universities and Colleges Union
UGC	University Grants Committee

1 Introduction

Why should anyone want to become an academic? It is certainly not an option that would maximize the lifetime income of a well-qualified and intelligent person. It is not a particularly high-status job, given that 'academic' is often used as a synonym for 'irrelevant'. At one time the role might have offered a considerable measure of professional autonomy and a relatively relaxed lifestyle for at least some individuals. However, as in other professions, a growing culture of regulation has reduced autonomy and added to the administrative burdens of academic work. The numbers and influence of administrators have grown, and with the growing influence of managerialism they are less likely to be the academics manqué of the past. Academic life is not exempt from the UK's long hours culture and evidence shows that most academics have to work well over the European Union's (EU) maximum 48-hour week to fulfil their roles of being researchers, teachers and managers. A persistent public myth is that periods like the summer 'vacation' are holidays when they are increasingly taken up by postgraduates, course preparation, various forms of summer teaching, let alone making progress on research.

▶ The satisfactions of an academic career

For all these drawbacks, many people still want to become academics, and our respondents emphasized how satisfying and fulfilling they had found an academic career. For most academics, there is still a sense of vocation about the job, even if it is being eroded. They may value a job that is intellectually challenging. They may consider that an academic post offers an opportunity to change the world for the better through influencing the clash of ideas or feeding into debates about public policy. Lucy, an English lecturer, illustrated some of the reasons that an academic career might seem uniquely attractive:

> I love literature and I work on the 19th century, which I think is a period which sees literature as about contributing to political change and that's why I did it

1

in terms of my politics. What I think attracted me to academia was that it did seem like a space that had still not been colonized by the capitalist ethic that lots of businesses had and that's why I feel it's so worrying now because that's obviously happened very quickly. But I still think there are spaces within it to opt out of that.

Although teaching can sometimes be frustrating, academics may enjoy the rewards that can come from a module that students both learn from and enjoy, or from contributing to the development of a particular student. A number of respondents emphasized the satisfactions that arose from connecting with students and helping their intellectual abilities. As Mike emphasized, 'The best aspect of my job is seeing a few students each year leave this institution having learnt something and having exceeded what I thought their abilities were when they came here.' Satisfaction may even be found from undertaking an administrative task proficiently or later in a career from the demanding roles of running a department or chairing a university committee. What Ian described as 'the flexibility to have what feels like several different jobs' may itself be an appealing aspect of academic work.

Whatever aspects of the job academics particularly enjoy, they may be people particularly inclined to a holistic view of life, which places more emphasis on non-material rewards and psychological satisfactions (which isn't to say that they wouldn't like better pay). Real satisfaction can be derived from a sense of purpose and belonging which an academic community can still provide, even if universities can look increasingly like educational service businesses run as impersonal bureaucracies. In this book we seek to explore issues that are generic to all academics in the humanities and social sciences, no matter where they work, although we are sensitive to the fact that there are some issues that are influenced by institutional affiliation. Academic life in the UK is becoming more stratified, although often in a rather complex way, so that there is considerable variation within the categories of both older and post-1992 universities.

This book does not seek to argue that an academic career can be 'managed' in some preordained way, that one can choose between a number of clearly marked-out career paths just as one might choose between a variety of alternative forms of mortgage. As Craig commented, 'I don't feel that I chose an academic career, I feel that it chose me at some level.' Most academic careers develop organically and serendipity plays an important role, although a number of respondents commented that they came from teaching or academic families and this influenced their choice of career. Some respondents had made their decision to become academics at a relatively early age, with Ann knowing from 14 or 15 that she wanted to work on a particular period of history. For others, the choice of career came later and was more accidental. Emma said in her interview, 'I don't think that I ever made a conscious decision to become an academic, it just happened. My tutor suggested I might do a master's and I didn't really know what else I wanted to do.'

Our respondents varied considerably in terms of their level of long-term ambition, ranging from Luke with a particular target date for a personal chair to Zoe who was more concerned about the overall balance of her life. For a career entrant, the only goals that are relevant may be immediate ones such as securing one's first permanent job, getting one's first research grant or writing a first book. Some of these new entrants will eventually become vice-chancellors, but anyone who sets that as a goal as a new lecturer is more likely to fail than to succeed. Becoming a professor is a more realistic goal, but a more immediate target may be a permanent lecturing position.

Academic life may be seen by others as not being a permanent career option, but something they shift in and out of, perhaps working at other times for a non-governmental organization, a museum, an archive or an international body. Some individuals like to have long-term goals and to think about how they are going to achieve them. Asked for the one piece of advice he would give a new entrant, Luke commented, 'Have a sense of what you want to achieve, try and set yourself goals, try to be aware of what are the most effective ways to do that.' Others are happy to see how life unfolds and what opportunities it presents. Emma remarked, 'I don't really think about career in terms of status and promotion. I just feel that I want to remain happy and continue to enjoy what I do.' Those in the second category may be just as 'successful' in objective terms and may be more comfortable in their own skins.

▶ The broader purposes of an academic career

Nevertheless, it is helpful to have some idea of why you are in academic life, even if you drifted into it through a series of chances, and what you want to achieve in terms of personal satisfaction. As Mike noted, 'I chose to study philosophy because I thought it would open myself as an individual to the world.' Ever since Newman's *The*

Idea of a University was published in 1853 (Newman, 1982), there has been debate about the purpose of a university in a modern society. In general terms, what Newman argued for was that a university offered 'a continuing process of intellectual reflection on what had already been perceived' (Barnett, 1990, p. 20). Members of universities engage in a continuous process of critical thinking about the world as a biosphere and an economic and social entity, the place of humanity (and other species) within it and their interactions with each other. This should lead to a process of 'intellectual self-empowerment' (Barnett, 1990, p. 21), which is beneficial for both the individual and the wider society. What has changed since Newman wrote this is that a university education has come to be seen less as an activity that can only be undertaken by a narrowly defined élite, and more as one that should be extended to as many people as possible who can benefit from it. There is no magic formula to determine what this figure should be, but 21st-century higher education policy emphasizes widening access and participation.

What has gained ground is what has been termed an instrumental or functionalist view of higher education. 'It includes the tendency to understand higher education in terms of the values and goals of the wider society, and the drive to evaluate the effectiveness of higher education in terms of its demonstrable impact on the wealth-generating capacity of society' (Barnett, 1990, p. 4). Particularly when it commands a substantial share of public funds, higher education has a responsibility to contribute to wider social goals, which can include meeting particular needs for qualified personnel. However, it is also necessary to maintain some boundaries between the academy and the wider society, without retreating into what is mistakenly called an 'ivory tower'. Higher education is 'more than just a sub-set of the education system' (Barnett, 1990, p. 7). Above all, it is important to retain standards of intellectual integrity in both research and teaching and to avoid subservience to vested interests. As Mike expressed it, 'The goal of this level of education is to produce people that are independent thinkers, critically analysing material.'

This process of criticism and analysis involves prevalent orthodoxies being constantly challenged, and this is as true of reflections about the nature and purpose of higher education as it is in any discipline taught in a university. Lists of core values in higher education (Barnett, 1990, pp. 8–9) are hence themselves open to challenge and many of them are highly contested concepts. 'The pursuit of truth and objective knowledge' (Barnett, 1990, p. 8) might seem beyond contention, given that no one would advocate that universities should engage in the promotion of deceit. But what is objective knowledge? Social constructivists would argue that all knowledge originates from social interaction, and individuals and groups construct their perceived reality. 'Rationality' (Barnett, 1990, p. 9) might seem to be a self-evident requirement, and is of key importance in the discipline of economics, but does such an approach take sufficient account of emotional intelligence? 'Academic freedom' (Barnett, 1990, p. 8) might seem essential to the functioning of a university, but should it be extended to racists who would deny access to a university education to ethnic minority groups? Readers of this book need to reflect on questions like these in order to shape a wider understanding of their purpose in being members of a university.

▶ The challenges of contemporary academic life

It is a common human ambition, particularly for the well educated, to want to 'make a difference' in one's life. Making a positive contribution to the lives of others can be an important source of personal satisfaction. However, life also presents us with increasingly more complex choices and challenges, not least because of technological change. We live in a world in which electronic technology facilitates 24/7 working, and for academics the boundaries between work and the rest of life are particularly blurred. There is always a risk of their work taking over their life to the exclusion of a proper work–life balance, a situation that makes them obsessive individuals who lose a sense of balance and proportion, and that is destructive to family and personal relationships. Ann recalled that a relationship with a partner that had been leading to marriage broke up largely because of the stress of both of them having short-term academic contracts: 'It's very difficult to have any sort of permanence [in one's life], I never know where I will be in 12 months' time. That is what I found most difficult and I know that other women of my age do as well.' She suggested that these pressures were particularly acute for women as child bearers.

Academics at the beginning of the 21st century in UK universities face an increasingly pressurized environment. A PhD student commented that he found academics in his department under 40 much more competitive and abrasive than those over 40. In broad terms, this is the generation who came into academic life at the time when research assessment exercises (RAEs) started to make a major impact. Luke commented, 'You're permanently moving in an environment of external audit of various kinds. External bodies define what a good academic is. There's that constant set of external imperatives.' Successive RAEs have led to an increasing emphasis on producing a given number of pieces of research output, preferably refereed journal articles in leading journals or monographs published by leading publishers, within a limited time period. Particularly following the financial settlement after the 2002 RAE which removed funding from departments graded as 3A and unexpectedly reduced the funding available to Grade 4 departments, there has been an increasing tendency towards the concentration of research in a relatively limited number of institutions. This has meant that departments not receiving research funding have increasingly faced either closure or merger as subordinate components of other departments, or have effectively been converted into teaching-only departments in which any research has to be undertaken as a spare-time leisure activity with no support in terms of funds or time set aside for research purposes. Many academics in the humanities and social sciences consider that they have suffered from the applicability of an inappropriate research funding model derived from the natural sciences to their subjects, although it is natural science departments in subjects such as chemistry that have been particularly susceptible to closure because of their higher running costs. Concentration of research funding may be necessary in the natural sciences because of the considerable cost of the equipment and laboratories needed for research, but social science is inherently less expensive.

There may, of course, still be benefits from having a critical mass of researchers in one location in terms of opportunities for research cooperation, seminar series and the attraction of visitors from overseas. It is easy to slip into believing that universities before the RAE existed in a golden age that permitted the leisurely pursuit of ideas for their own sake. Moran comments (2005, p.4), 'The world of the Research Assessment Exercise has led to the extinction of many life forms in academia. The disappearance of some – freeloaders, idlers, chancers – is welcome.' It should be remembered that public money was being made available for research and it was clear that many lecturers were not undertaking any serious research. Nevertheless, entrants to most academic departments today face an environment in which they are expected to generate an acceptable level and quality of research output quickly, as well as taking the first steps towards obtaining their own research funding.

These research goals have to be pursued in a climate in which greater attention is paid to excellence in teaching and its measurement through external quality assessment exercises of various kinds. New entrants will generally be expected to undertake a formal course in teaching techniques. This can confer many benefits, and is an advance on a situation where new entrants faced no training at all. However, it increases the time burdens that they face at an early stage of their career. Our respondents were also sceptical about the quality of many of those courses. New entrants to academia are also facing a situation in which students (and their parents) will be paying considerably more for their education than in the past. Open days have changed over the years from events at which 17 year olds sized up the accommodation and the social facilities (which they no doubt still do) to occasions when they are accompanied by parents seeking value for their money. Students are understandably going to require consistently high standards of teaching, are likely to make greater demands on staff time and to complain if they are not satisfied or even resort to litigation. Parents are taking an increasingly active interest in the higher education their children receive and whether it offers value for money. All this contributes to a more demanding environment for staff. As one respondent commented, 'In the early years, whether we like it or not, the job does take up a lot more time than it should. One has to expect to be working at weekends and in the evenings.'

The challenges offered by teaching are reinforced by the fact that the student population is becoming more socially diverse and heterogeneous. The quality of UK universities has always attracted students from overseas, but 40 years ago they were an exotic minority. At the postgraduate level 37 per cent of research students in 2003–4 were from outside the UK, up from 32.5 per cent in 1998–9. The number of non-UK postgraduate research students is expected to grow by 4 per cent a year while UK research student numbers are static or declining (*Times Higher Education Supplement*, 17 September 2004). At MA level, many courses are populated predominantly by students from outside the UK, often from China or elsewhere in East Asia. Different cultural backgrounds may mean that additional effort and energy has to be expended on issues such as explaining and monitoring plagiarism, although the more cosmopolitan character of courses offers new opportunities for teaching and learning. Although fewer undergraduate students are from outside the UK, some universities have attempted to tap this market by setting up overseas campuses. More new entrants in future could find themselves teaching in UK-run institutions located outside the UK.

The composition of the domestic student population, still largely drawn from the more prosperous sector of the population, will also change as the government's target of a 50 per cent participation rate is approached. Although the impact of this change has been most marked in the post-1992 universities, more traditional universities will also be required to recruit from those with social backgrounds where a university education has been a rarity. A more heterogeneous university population necessitates new approaches to learning, a need reinforced by the tendency for students to define themselves as consumers. A survey of 300 academics under the age of 40 found that nearly four out of five interviewed said that students expected far more help than when they were students (*Times Higher Education Supplement*, 17 September 2004). Expertise in the subject will need to be matched by an ability to communicate effectively in a way that fulfils learning objectives and the requirements of a more instrumental student population. Students will expect the effective use of information technology and virtual learning techniques, although they still value personal contact with teachers.

New entrants clearly need to approach academic life with as few illusions as possible. Colleagues may present as many problems as students. In one of our interviews, Lauren, a highly successful young academic who said that she loved her work, nevertheless suggested that academic life was highly competitive, often characterized by back-biting and notable for a reliance on often unpleasant gossip. Collegiality was more noticeable by its absence than its presence. Departments and disciplines may vary in this respect, with some friendlier and more supportive than others. As Luke commented, 'I think that collegiality is important. I think that departments that work well tend to be collegial.' Nevertheless, Lauren's comments may point to an essential truth about academic life. As she noted, 'you push yourself up by knocking others down'. American literature on higher education refers to an increasing 'hollowed collegiality' at departmental level as a consequence of increased competition and marketization, although these writers also suggest that Quality Assurance Agency (QAA) processes are actually beginning to build up collegiality again (see Massy, 2003).

In their role as researchers, academics could be conceptualized as being entrepreneurs running a one-person business where the product is ideas. Many small businesses (for example, hairdressers) operate in very localized markets in which the price and quality competition they face is readily evident, but academics are operating in an international market, which is particularly competitive in the UK because of the pressures generated by research assessment. It has many of the characteristics of a luxury goods market in that there are relatively few buyers and sellers and competition is based more on quality of output than its maximization. Reputation in the market is hence very important in determining who succeeds and who fails (it is more like running a specialist art gallery than a hairdressing salon). However, in universities the international character of the market and its ill-defined boundaries mean that participants are operating on the basis of imperfect information and in conditions of considerable uncertainty. If one accepts the proposition that an important motivation in any market is to reduce uncertainty, gossip is one mechanism for increasing the stock of information available, even if the quality of that information is unreliable.

This book recognizes that there are many and increasing challenges and problems in academic life. The structure of a career has changed substantially. As Gordon notes (2005, p. 41):

> Put simply, the career life cycle of many researchers increasingly does not match the simple 'classic' model. It remains true that the keystone of the fabric of the development of the scientific community is founded upon the training or apprenticeship experienced during the acquisition of the doctorate. However important caveats to that generalisation include historical differences between disciplines, inter-national variations between higher education systems, fluctuations in supply and demand in specific subsectors of the market for researchers, and the significant growth of praxis-based disciplines within the higher education sector.

It is no longer a case, if it ever was, of completing a PhD and then finding a job in which one remains for many years. Today's new academics are likely to move around a great deal before they attain a permanent position in a department of their liking. A much longer chain of appointments is likely than in the past. This is not necessarily undesirable, as it is possible to become stale and insufficiently challenged and stimulated if one remains in the same post for too long.

Once in a post, academics are required to simultaneously be successful teachers, cutting-edge researchers and to show an aptitude for an increasing burden of management and administration. Moreover, as Lauren noted, 'Working conditions are poor, salaries are poor, the resources we need to do our job are inadequate.' Yet she also remarked, 'I couldn't think of anything [else] I preferred to do.' For all the increasing pressures, an academic career still has many attractions, not least to engage in a process of intellectual discovery and convey those ideas to others. Working in a post-1992 university, Craig commented, 'I'm very glad all the time and very happy to be working in what I'm working in.' Our respondents had not generally thought seriously about switching careers, nor did they regret their career choice. That this finding is not atypical is confirmed by the fact that in the survey of young academics under 40, two-thirds said that they would be happy for their children to become academics. Just one in seven was actively contemplating a job outside the higher education sector and 85 per cent were committed to universities (*Times Higher Education Supplement*, 17 September 2004).

Academic life can be demanding in terms of time and effort, but it can also bring its own unique rewards. Comparable intellectual challenges and rewards are found in few other jobs; working with students can sometimes be draining or exasperating, but can also bring a real sense of achievement; and, although professional autonomy has been eroded, there are more opportunities to shape and plan your own career path than in most professions.

This book is not intended to dissuade anyone from pursuing an academic career, but to identify some of the challenges likely to be encountered and to provide guidance on ways of meeting them. Sometimes this will involve specific tips, sometimes more general suggestions on approaches to be adopted. There is no blueprint that can be applied to meet all circumstances. Each individual's experience is different in terms of career path, university, discipline and the person's own personal goals. There is, however, sufficient common ground to make reflection on the experience worthwhile. Academic life is as much a way of 'being' as it is 'doing' things, but equally the role can be broken down into a number of identifiable components and aspects, and it is these that are tackled in the succeeding chapters.

2 Getting a Job

The apprenticeship served before an academic job is secured can seem to be increasingly long and gruelling, although it is possible to draw too strong a contrast with a golden age that never really existed. Asked about the key challenges encountered in a contemporary academic career, Amy responded:

> All these things that didn't used to exist when I've spoken with professors who started 30 years ago, they walked into jobs basically, here and in the United States. It was very pleasant, they had time to write their thesis, it was time that was given over and you didn't do any teaching and you didn't have to do anything except be dedicated to that. Now when you start a master's programme, you're expected to publish, conference, network, all of those things.

After an undergraduate degree, it is increasingly customary to take a MA that involves some systematic research training. A PhD is then embarked on, but its completion will normally take four years. Given that a break may have been taken to explore the world or accumulate funds, it is not unusual for aspirant academics to be approaching 30 before they obtain a permanent post. In the meantime, they will have built up substantial debts, which they will have tried to contain by undertaking hourly-paid seminar teaching for their department or working as a tutor in a hall of residence. The teaching experience is valuable and necessary and enhances their chance of obtaining an appointment, but it can be time-consuming and distracts from the completion of the PhD.

Then, of course, there are opportunities to help with the organization of a workshop or a conference for the department, offering the chance not just to make some more money, but also possibly to network with leading figures in the profession. Such a task can, however, be demanding and frustrating, and easily lead to a further delay in the completion of the PhD. It is difficult to turn down a request from the department to assist with an event, but it is also a good time management technique to learn to say 'no' at an early stage of one's career.

The general point being made here is that it is very easy to become distracted from the principal goal of securing the kind of permanent academic job that you want. It is not a good experience to find that you have crossed some age threshold such as 30 to find that you are still deeply in debt, have held only a succession of part-time or temporary posts, and are still some way off completing your PhD. If you are happy in your department with your part-time teaching, and have a comfortable post in a student hall of residence which means that you have no accommodation costs, it is very easy to become institutionalized and almost to lose touch with the passage of time. The lack of challenge may almost be reassuring until one day you wake up and find that everyone in the PhD cohort you started with has secured a permanent job. It may be that you then decide it is an acceptable outcome to become the first departmental administrator educated to PhD level, but it is unlikely that this is the goal you had in mind when you first started your PhD.

Many of the most important decisions we take in our lives, such as meeting and selecting a partner, are the result of serendipity and chance. In our careers, there is nothing wrong with taking advantage of opportunities that suddenly emerge and just feel 'right'. Intuition is an important gift that should not be neglected and can often be relied upon. However, for most young entrants to academic life finding the right position involves quite a long search process which involves ranking different alternatives. It is therefore important to be clear about what you want from your first job. Most entrants do not obtain a position close to their ideal until their second or third career move, but even though it may be necessary to initially accept second or third best solutions, it is still a good idea to have some notion of where you would ultimately like to be. It is best not to rush into a job just because it is available and will solve your immediate financial problems.

▶ Some key choices: the choice of university

Three considerations are important in evaluating a post:

- the university
- the department
- personal considerations such as partner's location.

Jonathan Nicholls, registrar at the University of Birmingham, has predicted a trend of increased stratification of UK higher education in the five years from 2005, with institutions focusing more specifically on either teaching or research or seeking a 'niche' in the market (*Times Higher Education Supplement*, 8 July 2005). It is evident that some post-1992 universities have focused on a teaching role, particularly one with a social inclusion agenda and on provision for the local community. Research activity in such institutions may be concentrated in areas where there is real and distinctive strength, with the workload of the majority of staff making no provision for research activity, perhaps reinforced by devices such as central control of teaching timetables.

There are now many different league tables that attempt to rank universities in the UK. There are many subtle gradations, with the most obvious division between pre-1992 universities and those that were originally polytechnics or colleges of higher education. Among the pre-1992 universities, those universities that regard themselves as the leading research universities are organized in the Russell Group (see Table 2.1). Whether everyone would agree with this self-selected categorization is another matter; the important point is that it reflects and affects the orientation of these universities. It certainly was a categorization that impressed some of our respondents, with Ann, a senior lecturer in her twenties in a post-1992 university, aspiring to work in a Russell Group institution. These universities do account for over 60 per cent of the UK universities' research grant and contract income. In the 2001 RAE, 78 per cent of the staff in Grade 5* departments were located within Russell Group universities. Within this group, however, there is a further distinction between the 'golden triangle' universities of Oxford, Cambridge and London, and the rest. A world ranking of universities placed Oxford and Cambridge in sixth place, with the London School of Economics and Imperial College the next UK institutions in 11th and 14th place respectively. Three of the other institutions from the UK in the top 100 were London colleges (University College, the School of Oriental and African Studies and King's College London) (*Times Higher Education Supplement*, 5 November 2004). Outside the Russell Group, there is another grouping of smaller research universities, organized through the 1994 Group (see Table 2.2).

Within the post-1992 universities, there are some institutions that have placed considerable emphasis on developing research capacity, if not across the board, at least in certain selected subjects. There are others that focus on teaching, where research is relegated to an activity to be pursued in the academic's spare time. It is important for the career entrant to be sensitive to the differences among the post-1992

Table 2.1 Russell Group membership (2004)

University of Birmingham	London School of Economics
University of Bristol	University of Manchester
University of Cambridge	University of Newcastle upon Tyne
Cardiff University	University of Nottingham
University of Edinburgh	University of Oxford
University of Glasgow	University of Sheffield
Imperial College, London	University of Southampton
King's College London	University of Warwick
University of Leeds	University College London
University of Liverpool	

Table 2.2 Universities in the 1994 Group

Birkbeck, London	London School of Economics *
University of Bath	University of Reading
University of Durham	Royal Holloway, London
University of East Anglia	University of St Andrews
University of Essex	University of Surrey
University of Exeter	University of Sussex
Goldsmiths College, London	University of Warwick *
Lancaster University	University of York

Note: * Also in the Russell Group.

universities, with a number developing research profiles better than those of some less successful older universities. Some also have difficulty in recruiting enough students of a reasonable quality, not necessarily because of the quality of the institution itself, but because it has a location that is unattractive to students. Craig had recently made a deliberate move from a less well-regarded to a more highly rated post-1992 university and was very aware of the contrast:

> What's been striking for me over the last year is how the key challenges differ from institution to institution. At [former university] one of the key challenges was really about keeping one's job in an institution where student numbers were falling through the floor. It was really about adapting courses to the market place and every six months coming up with new courses, which were deemed to be appealing to the niche market that this month was the favourite

one for the executive. That was incredibly difficult, incredibly frustrating, less so for me as I sensed that if things fell into place I could always get out. One of the key challenges in new universities in English departments is falling student numbers.

It might seem that the ambitious academic should seek to work in a 'golden triangle' university. However, that choice is not as clear-cut as it might first appear. Oxford and Cambridge are still institutions based around their colleges, even if there is an effort to enhance the authority of the central university, an attempt that has met considerable resistance in Oxford. Colleges can vary considerably in the endowments available to them, despite the existence of mechanisms designed to bring about some equalization of resources. A collegiate environment can be very supportive, but it can also be difficult to adjust to for someone who has been used to a departmentally oriented environment. The tutorial system at Oxford and Cambridge is very labour-intensive and leads to contact hours that are much longer than in other research universities. Indeed, proposals have been made to halve the number of tutorials in English to relieve academics said to be 'worn down' by their workloads (*Times Higher Education Supplement*, 5 November 2004). Colleges can also generate quite a heavy administrative load and can have relatively convoluted decision-making processes. People who have come up through the Oxford and Cambridge system are often very keen to stay there, and find it difficult to adjust to different environments. Anyone who does not have an Oxford or Cambridge background may find the transition costs of adjustment to an appointment there quite high.

Lucy spent time at Oxford as a postgraduate research fellow and came away with mixed feelings about the university:

> My post-doc was fantastic, it gave me lots of time to research and Oxford is a very rich university, which supported that fully in a way that I imagine some places would not be able to. I think that it very problematically opens doors where it probably shouldn't. Even though I had a great time there, I think it's as good a university as anywhere else, but it has a cultural capital that certain places recognize and I'm very aware of that and I think it's problematic.

Perhaps then an attractive solution is to apply to one of the leading London colleges? For some disciplines a particular advantage of being located in London is relatively easy access to the British Library or the National Archives at Kew. The UK is still a highly centralized and metropolitan country, even allowing for devolution to Wales and Scotland,

and being in London gives you easy access to the top decision makers and the major centres for the arts and media. London is the location where seminars that bring academics and practitioners together are most likely to be held (although Edinburgh offers similar attractions in Scotland). However, operating a university in London is very expensive because of the cost of property and other additional costs such as enhanced security (although that is also an issue for some provincial universities). This can mean that your office will probably be more cramped than elsewhere and there may be more restrictions on access to it. It is a recurrent complaint that the salaries offered to support staff in London colleges often attract less capable or dedicated employees than can be recruited outside London. Above all, their high cost base can mean that London colleges are subject to recurrent financial crises. You also need to bear in mind the much higher cost of living in London, including property and commuting costs, which are not offset by the relatively small London allowance. One young lecturer in a London college recalled that, after purchasing a flat in one of the few inner London locations that he could afford, he received an early visit from the police to install a surveillance camera to monitor the activities of local criminal gangs.

Perhaps the ideal solution is then an ambitious research university located outside London but within easy reach of it (including Scottish universities that benefit from easy access to an airport with cheap flights). For example, given a free choice, one might consider the merged and highly ambitious University of Manchester, ranked at 43rd in the world rankings, or Edinburgh ranked at 48th. The major provincial universities have access to substantial resources and can provide a highly supportive environment for young scholars. However, the new entrant will be in a highly competitive environment in which internal promotion decisions will involve ranking high achievers against each other. Universities in this group quite reasonably expect high standards of performance from their employees, not just in terms of research output, but also excellence in teaching and an effective contribution to administration.

One of the smaller or less high-ranking research universities might therefore seem appealing, particularly if it has aspirations to improve its status. The 1994 Group defines itself as being made up of 'small and medium-sized universities' that 'are research universities of international standing'. This is defined in terms of 95 per cent of the staff *submitted* (our italics) to the 2001 RAE being in Grade 4 departments of above 'which indicates that member universities consistently employ researchers of a national or international standard' (http://www.1994group.ac.uk/level1/About.htm, 30 January 2005). In other words, these universities generally contain fewer 5* departments. Hence, the funds at such institutions may be more limited and what is available might be devoted to attracting 'star' professors who can boost research rankings. The aspirations of such institutions may exceed their ability to meet them, leading to younger members of staff being given a heavy workload and limited resources, yet still expected to meet high expectations. Sir Howard Newby, then chief executive of the Higher Education Funding Council, referred to smaller research universities as 'the squeezed middle', and there have been suggestions that they are particularly vulnerable to job cuts as they seek to restructure in anticipation of the 2008 RAE (*Times Higher Education Supplement*, 10 December 2004). These disadvantages may, however, be offset if the institution concerned has a highly ranked department in your own research area.

Many new entrants obtain their first appointment in a post-1992 university. They may see such an appointment as a staging post until they can obtain a position in a more highly ranked university. However, the risk is that the workload they encounter will prevent them finishing their PhD as quickly as they would wish or preparing the publications that will give them an impressive RAE entry. At worst, they might find themselves trapped in an institution with an intrusive management, low-quality students and a burdensome workload. Zoe commented of her experience at a post-1992 university, 'One of the differences is to do with the standard of students, obviously the entry criteria are rather different and we do end up having to take students whose academic abilities and interest in the course is perhaps rather below what we would like.'

Other disadvantages may include no or limited funds for research travel, no sabbatical leave arrangements, longer teaching hours than in other universities, limited support staff, an intrusive administration and shared offices.

However, there may be situations where securing an appointment in a post-1992 university is the right strategy to follow. First, there may be cases where a post-1992 university has a research strength in the area in which you specialize. Second, there are instances where post-1992 universities recruit younger staff with the expectation that they will build up a group that will add to the university's research strength. They are then given the opportunity to lead their own research group at a much younger age than would normally be the case. Although such a path can bring substantial rewards at an early age, it is a high-risk strategy. The overall culture of the university may not be support-ive to research and expectations of the timescale in which you can build an effective research group may be unrealistic. There may be a considerable emphasis on attracting external funding at the expense of other goals. Nevertheless, one can point to cases where this has been a very successful career strategy for a younger staff member. Third, you may be one of those who decide that they value teaching over research and in particular are interested in an institution that seeks to reach out to groups often excluded from higher education and offer them learn-ing opportunities. A post-1992 university may also be more interested in innovative methods of learning. If your preferences are in this direc-tion, a post-1992 university may be the place for you. Fourth, if you are interested in a career in university management, a post-1992 university may offer more opportunities at an earlier age.

Amy found that a position at a post-1992 university offered all sorts of opportunities that were not available at a leading research univer-sity. She worked on a series of temporary contracts for a research university and put forward a proposal for a writing centre to offer tuto-rials to students. After 18 months, the proposal was rejected, but a similar position became available at a post-1992 university, which she obtained. It was even better as it was linked with a senior management position and offered a combination of management, teaching and research.

▶ Working outside the UK

Another option is to work outside the UK. There may be personal considerations that affect such a choice. Leaving those aside, and assuming that you have the linguistic skills, universities elsewhere in Europe (even allowing for variations between countries) operate in a very different context in terms of degree structure, modes of exami-nation and attitudes towards students than in the UK. North Ameri-can universities may appear to offer the advantage of operating in a similar language (except in Quebec), but also differ in terms of degree structure and student expectations, including a much greater willingness to attempt to 'negotiate' grades. Disciplinary environ-ments may also be different: for example, American political science is more quantitative in orientation than its UK counterpart. The resource-rich environment of the better North American universities has its attractions, but it should be remembered that liberal arts colleges are very demanding in terms of the amount of time expected to be devoting to teaching.

Universities in Australia and New Zealand are probably among the closest to the UK model, which helps to explain why there is such active two-way traffic in academic staff between Australasia and the UK. However, the long flights necessary to overcome geographical isolation are a problem in terms of maintaining a research profile.

Many native Australians seek to negotiate solutions that split their careers between Australia and the UK. Before making any decision to take a job outside the UK, you need to think about how you would react to it becoming permanent in both personal and career terms. If you think you would like to come back at some point, make sure that you have an effective strategy that would enable you to do so. For example, work on Australian themes published in Australian journals may not be rated as highly as perhaps it should be in the UK.

Working as an academic in Germany

A university elsewhere in Northern Europe may be an option that interests those with the relevant linguistic skills and may offer opportunities to develop a research speciality. The 1999 Bologna Declaration and developments that have followed from it are designed to make degree structures at undergraduate and postgraduate level more convergent across European countries and also to introduce more international convergence in external quality assurance. This should in time make the prospect of working in Europe a more inviting one. Southern European universities are often still based around patron–client relationships centred on a professor and his or her group. National systems of recruitment, as in Italy, may lead to new entrants trained in Milan being dispatched to Trieste, Sardinia or Sicily. The university system in Germany offers an example of a continental system that may appeal to some UK career entrants. In terms of publication citations, it ranks third in terms of research behind the US and the UK (Gruss, 2005, p. 5). A considerable amount of research in Germany is conducted in research organizations, notably the Max-Planck-Gesellschaft (made up of 78 institutes and 12,153 staff in 2005), but also other research institutes such as the Wissenschaftszentrum in Berlin, which employs 140 social scientists to undertake basic social science research. Although the Max-Planck-Gesellschaft was historically associated with the natural sciences, it has a particular interest in interdisciplinary work and a considerable strength in the social sciences. Its research perspectives include ageing, health, social order in a global world, and markets and institutions (Max Planck Society, 2005). Among its research institutes are ones specializing in law, history (including specialized coverage of European legal history and the history of science) and art history (located in Rome). More recently, the federal government has initiated a financial package to enable universities to create German equivalents of Oxford or Harvard. There is also a trend to undertake more teaching in English to appeal to the international market.

Education in Germany is the sole responsibility of the Länder (provincial governments), so higher education can differ somewhat from state to state. A basic federal framework law (the Hochschulrahmengesetz) is decided jointly between the Länder and the federal government to provide common standards in terms of employment and career progression (there is no equivalent legislation in the United States). Universities are directly responsible to the relevant state education ministry, which has the formal responsibility of appointing staff. Occasionally, political considerations have intruded in decisions by the responsible land minister.

In Germany you need two doctorates to become a full professor, the second being known as the Habilitation. It should be noted that a German doctorate is generally much shorter than a UK or American PhD and normally takes about two-and-a-half years to complete. The topics and questions are also usually provided by the supervising professor (or Doktorvater). This structure is a potential problem for recruits from abroad, and the recent introduction of the junior professorship is an attempt to address this issue. However, not all of the Länder have supported the reform. For example, Berlin and Lower Saxony are introducing the junior professorship, but states such as Bavaria have been more reluctant.

PhD students in Germany usually get two-year posts at a university in order to pursue their degree. However, these posts are often on a part-time basis so that two PhD students share one full-time position. In most cases, they are in effect expected to work full time and do their research when they can, although this is not so different from the experience of PhD students occupying part-time posts in the UK. Career progression is difficult as substantial cuts in the education budgets of the Länder have resulted in very few jobs being available to build up a career as a researcher and/or lecturer. In particular, permanent positions have been sharply cut back, adding to a high degree of job insecurity and a reliance on short- to medium-term funding with no clear link to a career structure. The grass is certainly not greener in Germany than in the UK, and this is also true of a number of other continental European countries whose PhD graduates seek posts in the UK. Working elsewhere in Europe most often makes sense for research or personal reasons.

Another option is offered by the increasing trend, encouraged by government, for UK universities to open their own campuses in locations such as China, Malaysia, India and Singapore. Spending a couple of years in such a location may be beneficial, especially if there is some relationship with your own research interests. However, a contract that limits you to teaching on the remote campus, with no guarantee of returning to the UK site, may leave you trapped in a situation that is financially beneficial but makes it difficult for you to develop your research in the way that you would wish. There is also always the possibility of local partners of the university gradually acquiring a more dominant role in such arrangements, leading to a reduction in the need for expatriate staff, while sometimes such campuses may fail to be financially successful. However, as a matter of personal preference, an expatriate career pursued in a succession of locations may be attractive to some academics.

▶ The choice of department

Although you are a member of a university, the immediate environment in which you work is a 'department', however it is termed. By this is meant an organizational unit concerned with research and teaching in a discipline or related set of disciplines. The recent fashion in university management has been to combine 'departments' into 'schools', which have in any case often been the preferred form of organization in post-1992 universities. It is sometimes claimed that such a move offers economies of scale, but in fact its real gain from the point of view of a university's management may be increased opportunities for central control. A smaller number of heads of school who are dedicated line managers are easier to control than a larger number of heads of department who may see themselves as academics as much as managers. It is a good idea to have some understanding of the organizational structure that relates to a post for which you are applying. If you have interdisciplinary or multidisciplinary arrangements, a looser organizational relationship which places less emphasis on academic disciplines may suit you better. The highly ranked University of Sussex offers a good example of such an arrangement.

In general, however, whatever the terminology and organizational arrangements, you will be working alongside a group of colleagues in your discipline. Optimally, you should look for a department that has the following characteristics:

- It is of a reasonable size.
- It has a research group related to your interests (such a group may, of course, cross departmental boundaries).
- It should not be a department that is factionalized or has a reputation for poor relationships among colleagues.

If the department is too small (say, less than ten full-time members of staff), you may have to teach on a wide range of courses, not all of them related to your interests. The department may have little spare capacity to cover the departure or illness of a staff member, and the resultant burden may be placed on the most junior member of staff. The department may have difficulty in punching its weight in internal university politics. In an era of research concentration, the department may even be vulnerable to merger or closure. On the other hand, a department which is very large (say, over 30 staff) may be more impersonal and it may be more difficult for a new entrant to adjust to its culture and procedures. Emma noted, 'What surprised me when I came to a very large department was that there were some people you might not see for weeks on end because their teaching days are different from yours.' Some larger departments try to overcome this problem by organizing research groupings within them. This model is borrowed from the natural sciences where the laboratory provides a focus for interaction, but how well it works within the humanities and social sciences may depend on the personalities involved.

The advantages of having a research group close to your interests should be readily apparent. It will provide you with a group of colleagues who will be interested in your research, will be able to provide relevant mentoring and open doors for you to a range of research opportunities. If, on the other hand, you go to a department where no one else shares your speciality, you are likely to feel isolated, even if you have started to build your own networks and are in regular electronic communication with others who share your interests. Although academics are generally too busy to have leisurely lunches discussing their mutual interests of the kind that happened in senior common rooms in the past, even a snatched conversation in the corridor with a colleague or a chat over a glass of wine after a seminar with someone working in your area may yield considerable benefits. Considerations about the orientation of the department may be particularly important in a discipline such as philosophy, where there has been a sharp division between continental and analytic philosophy. Mike commented, 'There is a division and it does affect the discipline. The division was extremely dogmatic and people were very aggressive and dismissive of people who studied the other type of philosophy, but that's less the case now.'

Unfortunately, there are academic departments where long-standing disagreements between colleagues have produced factions that are engaged in a continuous internal war with each other. This may reflect genuine intellectual disagreements or it may have its origins in some long forgotten argument over a trivial matter. Academics can be difficult people to work with, and these issues are explored more fully in a later chapter. As a general principle, however, it is best to avoid departments where internal relationships are poor. As a new member of the department, the factions may compete for your allegiance, but once you join one of them, the other faction will be opposed to you. If you try to join none of the factions, you may find yourself isolated. Internal tensions within departments are one of the subjects of gossip among colleagues, and tales are often exaggerated in the retelling. Nevertheless, if different people that you think well of tell you that a particular department is beset with internal tensions, it is something you should bear in mind when applying for a job.

▶ Personal considerations

Personal considerations are important when you are deciding whether to apply for a job. These may vary from one person to another. If you are a native Welsh speaker, you might be particularly interested in obtaining a post at a Welsh institution. If your main leisure interest is mountaineering or hill walking, Essex might not be your favoured location. A respondent who worked in Northern Ireland pointed out, 'There is a different labour market in Northern Ireland which distorts things.' Academics from the UK mainland may be reluctant to relocate there for a variety of reasons while the proportion of academics from outside the UK may be higher than at other universities. In general young people with broad cultural and sporting interests are likely to find more to interest them in one of the major cities of the country. A pleasant medium-sized town may be an ideal location for a young family with children, but less suitable for a single person. It may also offer fewer job opportunities for a partner who is not an academic, and indeed some universities located away from big cities consider that this can affect recruitment and retention. Not all needs can be catered for, of course. Some undergraduates locate themselves in, say, Liverpool or Manchester so that they can actively support the football club they followed when they were growing up in Surrey. When it comes to choosing a job location, this is not a good basis for choice.

The really important and difficult consideration about applying for jobs is how they relate to where a partner is located. At one time universities used to insist that staff lived within a certain specified distance of the university. For example, the University of Oxford required that its academic staff lived within a certain distance of Carfax in the centre of the city. Indeed, an Oxford informant stated, 'Some of the individual colleges there provide their fellows with housing allowances, a form of pensionable supplement to salary. However they do require that to qualify for it you must be living in a named house that is within so many miles of Carfax.' However, in many institutions these requirements were never strictly enforced and often lapsed. They would not be really practical to enforce in contemporary conditions and in any case would not be compatible with employment law.

Dual careers mean that academics have become much more geographically dispersed in relation to their institutions. Sometimes it is possible to choose an intermediate location from which both partners in a relationship can undertake a long but tolerable commute to their jobs. This may be helped by the fact that university staff can work from home to some extent. In some cases universities may have accommodation where staff can stay for a couple of nights a week or colleagues may be willing to let you use a spare room on an occasional basis. However, sometimes the distance separating partners is so great that one of them has to be away most of the week. Even though email, text messages and mobile phones make regular communication easier and cheaper, it is not the same as being together on a regular basis. If two particular locations (say, Bristol and Newcastle) seem acceptable because they are linked by cheap flights, remember that the flights may become more expensive or withdrawn altogether, and you will be thrown back on an unreliable and overcrowded rail network that is particularly subject to disruption at weekends. The *Higher* highlighted the case of a young lecturer at Sheffield whose partner was at a Welsh institution, meaning that they had to live apart for most of the week and she had to face a four-hour train journey at the beginning and end of each week. She commented, 'My heart fills with dread at the thought of another long stretch away from my beloved. I hate being apart from him. I really enjoy being an academic, but it is exhausting being apart' (*Times Higher Education Supplement*, 13 February 2004).

Repeated separations can test a relationship, but the real difficulties can begin when children arrive. Let us suppose that one partner works in Bristol and the other in London and they live at a midpoint on the London–Bristol railway line such as Didcot. Any delay on the rail network and there is a real risk that they may incur the heavy fines that nurseries impose on parents who are even minutes late in collecting their children. Of course, when they embark on a separated relationship, many couples are optimistic that things will work out sooner or later and they will find jobs, if not in the same institution, at least at two that are within a reasonable distance of each other. However, the partner who moves may have to shift to a less desirable department or sacrifice opportunities for career advancement. If both partners move, they may both lose out. Individuals may find themselves faced with an unpalatable choice between their careers and their relationship.

What is evident is that your first job is unlikely to be your ideal one. As Ann noted, 'Academic jobs are so few and far between that I would take the first job that comes up.' So why not just accept the first offer that comes along? First, it is a waste of time applying for jobs for which you are not qualified. There is little point in a mediaeval historian applying for a post for a modern historian who can teach a module on inter-war dictatorships. If you apply for a job for which you are qualified but you do not really want because you do not like the institution or the department or it is hundreds of miles away from your partner, this will undoubtedly affect your preparation for the interview or your demeanour at it. As a consequence, you will probably not be successful anyway. What you do need to do is to seriously evaluate the advantages and disadvantages of any job for which you apply. For example, if you are an American literature expert and you apply for a job in a department whose focus is European literature, are the risks of isolation offset by the reputation of the university and the fact that it is within commutable distance of your partner?

You will have to balance a range of competing considerations and ultimately it is a decision that only you can make. It is, however, a good idea to think systematically about the relevant considerations and try to prioritize them. Consider a hypothetical example. Nicola is an expert on Icelandic sagas and her partner is a solicitor who lives in the

London area and works in a highly specialized area of law for which the main opportunities are in the capital. She hears on the grapevine that jobs at three institutions are to become available:

- The University of Thurso has the biggest concentration of Icelandic experts in the UK, including some of the leading experts on Icelandic literature. It was rated 5* in the last RAE. However, the department is split down the middle by a dispute over the correct form of translation from Icelandic. It is also very difficult to get from Thurso to London.
- The University of Skegness is a post-1992 institution, which has been attempting to develop a Nordic studies speciality. A 4 was obtained in the last RAE, but the university is willing to put more money in the area. However, Nicola would be the only Icelandic expert in the department where the main speciality is Norwegian studies. Skegness has poor road and rail communications with London.
- The University of Basildon has won a contract to provide training for public sector workers from Iceland and needs someone on its staff who knows Iceland and can speak Icelandic. It is an easy commute from London but the post is predominantly a teaching one and no entry will be made from the subject area for the next RAE. There is no one else in the university with an interest in Iceland or, for that matter, in literature more generally.

This is perhaps an extreme example of a dilemma that could be faced by any job applicant working in a minority subject. There are no 'right' answers to it. However, even before you begin your search process for a job you should be thinking of the key considerations that affect your choice. Otherwise you may find yourself in a post that is the wrong one for all sorts of reasons and could lead to a very unsatisfactory start to your career.

▶ The search process and the entry post

The process of job search begins long before you actually make a job application. As your PhD progresses, you will be making contacts with PhD students in other institutions through more or less formal networks (many professional associations have graduate sections). These contacts will help you to gain knowledge about other institutions in your subject area and what the departments are really like. You

will also be starting to make conference presentations, initially probably at conferences designed specifically for graduate students. These
conference presentations will make you known to academics in the
area and may lead to your first publications. It is also helpful to start
reading job advertisements well before you are ready to apply for them.
This will give you some idea of the state of the market, what kinds of
jobs are becoming available and what the requirements are for them.
The best place to look is online at www.jobs.ac.uk, which is well categorized by type of job and discipline. However, most jobs will also be
advertised either in the *Guardian* or in the *Times Higher Education
Supplement*.

Exactly when you start applying for jobs will be influenced by a
number of considerations, not least financial ones. However, if you
have a funded PhD, it is probably best to use the full extent of the funds
available before you apply for a post.

Many posts will require that you have a PhD or are very near completion. Even if they do not, it is possible to underestimate how hard it will
be to find time to work on your PhD in the first year of a teaching post
when you are writing new courses. The completion of the PhD may be
delayed, which can cause serious problems as many universities now
impose limits on the time that you are allowed to take. You may also
have difficulty in writing the publications necessary to obtain a better
or permanent post.

However, it is important not to be over-cautious. As Ruth stated:

> One piece of advice I saw was to look at the criteria in the advertisement and if
> you think you fit 60 to 70 per cent of those criteria, but don't fit the 30 to 40 per
> cent, then do not be put off by that. As long as you meet the majority of the
> criteria, then apply. Because so much of it depends upon the market for that
> particular job: who is applying, what the unstated agenda of the department is
> – and that's where speaking to people currently working in the department or
> who know the department is a good idea.

Different types of post: the post-doctoral fellowship

Relatively few young academics are fortunate enough to secure a post
that is in effect permanent, that is, subject to satisfactory completion
of probation, as their first appointment. For many of them the alternatives that are open to them are a post-doctoral research fellowship
(PDF), a contract research post, a temporary lectureship or a post that
is specifically designated as a teaching fellowship (although many
temporary lectureships are in effect teaching fellowships given the

workload involved). Each of these types of position has its advantages and disadvantages.

A PDF is in many ways the most advantageous of these posts. As Ann noted, 'A PDF is without peer, it sets you up for life.' It is usually associated with very limited or no teaching duties and no administrative burdens. It means that you have a period of time free from other distractions to produce publications from your PhD and also to start planning your next major research project. As a result you become much more attractive as a candidate for a post in a leading institution. The problem is that relatively few such posts are available. Oxford and Cambridge colleges have a number, and they are open to graduates of any university, but it is likely that most of them are taken by graduates of the universities concerned. The research councils, the British Academy and the Leverhulme have a limited number available, but they are very competitive. Moreover, attractive as such posts are, they are not without their disadvantages. Lucy noted, 'I think that having a post-doc is great for some people, I think that for other people it can provide a three-year space where you do nothing and become very disillusioned and I have seen that happen as well.' Amy advised, 'If you have a choice between a post-doc and a permanent job, take the permanent job. A post-doc is just another temporary measure.' You may also become too used to having all your working time to do your research.

Contract research

Contract research posts may offer a suitable entry route for some new academics, although they are more common in the social sciences than in the humanities. In 2002–3 there were nearly 46,000 research-only academics in UK universities, a third of all academics. Of these, 93 per cent were on fixed-term contracts (*Times Higher Education Supplement*, 4 February 2005). A project may arise in your own institution that is related to your own research interests and enables you to open up a new avenue of enquiry, or an opportunity may occur elsewhere. Contract research posts usually offer you the opportunity to publish from the project and thus improve your CV, although typically they are joint publications, which may diminish their value in the eyes of a prospective employer. Ann commented that a contract research post was 'the quickest way to end your career before it's even started because you end up doing someone else's book work and don't get to develop your ideas'. However, Mike was involved in helping with the editing of a book as a contract researcher, which enabled him to develop contacts with publishers and leading researchers. In the humanities in particular there are a number of contract research posts associated with teaching and learning projects that can add something extra to someone's range of experience. Balanced against an acquisition of additional skills, in say e-learning, on other projects you may find a lot of your time taken up with rather routine or mundane tasks such as processing or cataloguing data. Isolation from the rest of the department can be a real problem for contract researchers, especially if they are required to undertake prolonged periods of research away from the university in archives or in the field. In any event it is important to take any opportunities that arise to do some teaching while you are in a contract research post, otherwise a prospective employer may think that you have insufficient teaching experience to balance your research skills.

You also need to think very carefully about making a career out of being a contract researcher. This may seem to be an attractive prospect if it is research rather than teaching that attracts you in a university career. However, you will always be involved in projects that have, at least in part, been designed by others so you will not have the autonomy to develop your own particular interests. A career as a contract researcher can be insecure, and while institutions may provide 'bridging' funds to keep you in work for short periods of time between projects, a lot of your time will be taken up in the time-consuming task of writing applications for new grants. A study by John Hockey of the University of Gloucestershire of 60 contract researchers in the social sciences found that many of them had to work free in universities as a means of maintaining their contracts (*Times Higher Education Supplement*, 4 February 2005). Contract researchers also often complain with some justification that there is no real career structure for them in universities, which are organized around the assumption that the normal pattern is for staff to combine research, teaching and management roles. As they become more senior, universities may replace them with younger staff who cost less money.

Temporary lectureships and teaching fellows

For many new entrants, however, the most typical entry post is the temporary lectureship. From most of our respondents, this was seen as the typical entry route to an academic career. Amy noted:

> In English the route is you get a temporary job and eventually, hopefully, maybe, you get a permanent job and it doesn't have anything to do with any loyalty you have to an institution. I've seen a lot of people think 'I'm going to be really loyal to this institution', and the institution isn't going to do anything.

Temporary posts arise for a number of reasons, most usually because of the need to cover the teaching of a member of staff who is away on study leave, has taken up a research grant or is on maternity leave. Some posts do arise because many departments have greater financial autonomy and are prepared to commit to a temporary post in a particular area until their funding position becomes clearer. If possible it is helpful to find out why the post has arisen, as this will give you some information about whether it is likely to become permanent. Many posts are for one year only, or even for just nine months. Three-year posts used to be more common but changes in relevant legislation mean that universities have to either convert the post into a permanent one or make redundancy payments. Human resources departments will often recommend that someone who has had a succession of one-year posts should be made permanent.

Our respondents thought that there were both advantages and disadvantages to temporary posts. On the one hand, they provide training; on the other hand, either the permanent member of staff whose leave has created the vacancy will return or funds will become available to make the temporary post a permanent one, at which point a new field of candidates will appear, creating a tricky situation for both the appointing institution and the temporary lecturer. A clear disadvantage is that a temporary lecturer can be treated as a peripheral member of a department. Luke noted, 'Very often they are appointed to positions which are to plug gaps in teaching, the emphasis of what they are doing is teaching, so their capacity to become citizens of a department is not something that is automatically obvious.' However, he noted, 'I can think of cases where people have positioned themselves in such a way that they make themselves good citizens and to a degree indispensable.' Lucy, however, pointed out the difficulties of being a good citizen. 'If you are doing a two or three-year temporary position where you're very much part of the institution then it becomes quite difficult to commit. You want to commit but then if you commit too much, you're diverting from finding a permanent job.' Emma saw some positive advantages in temporary posts: 'if you end up having, say, two temporary appointments then you experience different places, different institutional cultures that bears fruit later on'. Against that set of advantages 'it has negative effects in terms of your family, your financial security and your ability to plan'. On balance, however, as Ruth noted, 'I think it is quite important in the long run to show you are willing to take a temporary post and make the necessary sacrifices if you actually want to end up in a permanent position.'

Temporary lecturers potentially have something of an advantage when posts become available in the department, although sometimes their inclusion on a short list may simply be a matter of courtesy rather than being placed in pole position. Indeed, internal candidates sometimes 'complain that they are disadvantaged because the interviewers know too much about them already' (Basnett, 2004a, p. 8). It is as well to bear in mind, however, that your chances of success may be affected by your own conduct as a temporary lecturer in the department. Eadie's (2005, p. 10) comment on teaching fellows also applies to temporary lecturers: 'Since teaching fellows are there to lighten the load of department, not add to it, independence, confidence and reliability are prerequisites.' A difficult balance has to be drawn between being seen as helpful and collegial, and avoiding being overloaded with burdensome tasks that no one else wants to undertake. It is as well to remember that there is another side of the coin to complaints by temporary staff about being exploited. Susan Basnett (2004a, p. 9) states, 'I hear a lot of complaints about fixed-term contract staff moaning about trivia, making unreasonable demands and trying to pull rank, particularly with secretaries and students.' She also offers some good advice to candidates hoping to turn a temporary post into a permanent one:

> The strong internal candidate comes with support from peers as well as a demonstrably strong CV. Nobody gets a job by just being a nice person, but it certainly helps, all other things being equal. Being difficult, standing on your dignity, refusing to go that extra yard or two will weigh heavily against you.
>
> (Basnett, 2004a, p. 11)

The title of teaching fellow for a post is an explicit recognition of what many temporary lecturers actually do, including such tasks as pastoral care, open days, dissertation supervision and administrative tasks. With more staff regularly on research leave in the run up to the RAE, the number of such posts has proliferated. As Eadie notes (2005, p. 10):

> While the post of teaching fellow is a significant improvement on that of part-time tutor in terms of pay and conditions, there are draw-backs. The first obvious draw-back is the temporary or rolling nature of many contracts which means economic insecurity ... Teaching fellows are vulnerable to poor student feedback and dispensable when contracts end.

▶ Making the application: the CV and the application form

Your curriculum vitae (CV) is a vital tool in your job search. You may wish to show it to prospective employers who could have a post in the future and it will often accompany a job application. It will also be needed for applications for research and conference travel grants. As Blaxter, Hughes and Tight note (1998, p. 39): 'Your curriculum vitae embodies a tension which will be present throughout your application – between, on the one hand, brevity and clarity, and, on the other, comprehensiveness.' The authors of an American handbook on an academic career suggest that:

> Members of the search committee usually do not have more than twenty seconds for the initial screening of a CV, so you do not have much time to introduce yourself, explain what your research is all about, and impress the reader that you are the one the department is looking for.
>
> (Goldsmith, Komlos and Gold, 2001, p. 82)

While one would hope that UK appointing committees would have a little more time than that to scan applications before assigning them to the reject pile, it is important to realize that decisions about appointments are made by very busy people often handling a large number of applications who necessarily read CVs quickly and critically. As Luke noted:

> In terms of CV construction one of the most annoying things when you confront one is not having a clear path to navigate through. You want pieces of information that you can ascertain quickly what the person's merits are, so you need to have a very clear idea of their academic history, their publications, their research profile, those kinds of things.

Most CVs submitted by new entrants include too much extraneous information, often giving the impression that they have been 'padded' to suggest more accomplishments than is in fact the case. Experienced selectors will soon pick this up: what they need to know is what your key strengths are. As Amy emphasized:

> Try not to put too much on it so that it looks neat and not crammed in with every little detail. One specific tip I was given when I came to the UK is if you are talking about different courses you have taught, put in a little 'in brackets'

giving 'average course size in numbers' because it's such a new thing here in the UK that you can teach more than ten students at once.

For some reason, perhaps because they want to demonstrate that they are balanced individuals with a range of interests, some applicants think that it is a good idea to insert information about unusual hobbies or even sports teams they support. There is then always a risk that selectors may think that the outside interests may consume too much of your time, or the fact that you like to make models of ships to put in bottles suggests an unusual or unduly introverted personality. Some hints on CV design are contained in Box 2.1, but the key to a good CV is the overall structure:

> However, you structure it, it is critical that anyone examining your curriculum vitae should be able to find their way around it quickly. So don't make it longer than necessary, include short summary sections, and lay particular emphasis on key aspects of your academic and work histories.
>
> (Blaxter, Hughes and Tight, 1998, p. 38)

For posts in most institutions, your research and publications record is going to be of key importance. Luke advised:

> Make sure that you are very clear about your publication profile; make that very visible. In a situation where you are confronted with, say, 70 applications for a lecturer post, the person reading those applications simply isn't going to have time to read everything in depth so you've got to be savvy about what any decent department wants, which is RAE product. So you have to make it clear that you have good pieces in situ or that you have a strategy over the relevant RAE cycle.

Luke added a note of warning, 'Often under the heading of publications there's a deconstruction job that has to be done, so don't put in book reviews, don't bump in things that are simply kind of twinkles in your eye.' One might add, however, that there are differences between disciplines in terms of what counts as a publication. In economics, where the emphasis is on publishing in leading refereed journals to the exclusion of almost everything else, a revise and resubmit from a major journal can be regarded as an achievement. In some humanities disciplines, a long book review in a well-regarded journal might count for more than it would in the social sciences. Above all, as Lauren emphasized,

Job applications are not only about what you have done, but what you are doing and will be doing. It's important that you give an idea that you have a dynamic research agenda and that it's evolving and you know where you are going.

Box 2.1 Designing your CV

What you should include

Key information about your academic career:

- Education from university level
- Main areas of research interest
- Research strategy over the next five years
- Publications (if you include submissions, make clear what stage they are at and whether you have a book contract)
- Employment experience, including details of courses taught and any examining work
- Conference presentations
- Grants and scholarships (include travel grants)
- For some humanities posts, for example, in media, film and theatre studies, information about relevant production experience
- Names of referees

You should also explain any gaps in your career. Explain what you were doing, for example, 'gap year'.

What you should omit

- Marital status, children
- Details of secondary education
- Publication plans, which do not have any basis, for example, in working papers
- Trivial media experiences (but include a major contribution to a programme or series even if you were just concerned with production planning)
- Unusual or time-consuming leisure interests
- Inaccurate, exaggerated or false statements

A clear indication must be given of what further research projects are to be pursued and how they will be undertaken.

You are not required to include in your CV information about marital status and children, which could be a basis for discriminating against a candidate. Unfortunately, even though the chair of a panel should intervene if such a consideration is raised, 'such information can come up for comment in a way that detracts from a candidate's appeal, especially if a candidate is female' (Goldsmith, Komlos and Gold, 2001, p. 79). Equally, your sexual orientation is irrelevant to whether you are qualified for a post. You are not required to include your date of birth, but it is possible for selection panels to infer this from the dates of your secondary education. 'Some people try to prevent age discrimination by not putting dates at all on their educational career, but that only tips people off that you're trying to disguise your age' (Goldsmith, Komlos and Gold, 2001, p. 83). Although this should not happen, late entrants to academic life may face hurdles that other candidates do not face, but even if you conceal information that relates to your age, it will be evident in broad terms if you are called for interview. What you cannot avoid accounting for are unexplained gaps in your career. These tend to bother selection panels, particularly if they follow completion of the PhD. It's probably 'better to let people know what you've been doing than to give them a gap that may fill them up with their uncomfortable imaginings' (Goldsmith, Komlos and Gold, 2001, p. 83).

A more general point is that CVs often provide too much information about secondary education. Panels are not going to make a decision based on how many GCSEs you passed or what A level grades you obtained, even though you may be proud of what you achieved in that respect. They are only interested in what happened from the time you started university. It may also be a hostage to fortune to include details of your secondary education, particularly if you went to an independent or a fee-paying school. The UK is much less divided on class grounds than it once was, but inverted snobbery has not disappeared and academics on panels may justify prejudices on meritocratic grounds of positive discrimination.

The letter that accompanies the application can be important as it can help to highlight your key strengths. Lucy recalled:

> As soon as I had my job letter sorted out, that's when I started to get short listed. I sense that all sorts of postgraduates all write a letter, which will say 'Dear university, I want to apply for this job.' The American university I was at

taught me to write about what my research goals were, what my teaching methodology was, how I saw myself in relation to the profession.

CV construction is an area where it is particularly important to seek advice, particularly given that UK universities are probably not as good as their American counterparts in providing systematic training on this subject. Look at the CVs of other new entrants and more senior members of the profession. Many examples are available on the Internet, but also ask members of your department if you can see their CVs. Submit your CV for comment to your peers, but also to mentors and supervisors. While you should have a generic CV as a template, adjust it to reflect the particular specification of the job for which you are applying and the interests of the department, without making claims that cannot be justified. However, although presentation is important, it will not compensate for a lack of substance. It is building the CV rather than designing it that is important.

University job application forms sometimes apply to a range of posts and may ask for information that appears to be irrelevant to an academic post, for example, whether you have a clean driving licence. However, this may be relevant if you have to drive students in a minibus for field trips or if the job is a research position that involves visits to a wide geographical range of locations to conduct interviews. Even if you do not want to own a car yourself, a driving licence is a useful life skill and it is surprising (or perhaps not) how many academics lack it. In any event, make sure that you fill in the form completely, even if some of the questions seem irrelevant, as a failure to complete may be interpreted as evidence of carelessness or a casual approach to the post being applied for.

One of the key choices you have to make about job applications is about who you should name as referees. For most posts, three names are required, for others two. Surprisingly, this is an area in which candidates sometimes make basic mistakes. As Luke emphasized:

> Make sure your referees are credible. I've seen some hilariously inept applications. Referee 2 is a train driver. Be sufficiently well networked to have three decent referees to call, preferably to indicate that you are somebody who is known in the profession somewhere. That's extremely important.

You may have already selected a standard set of referees and named them on your CV. Normally, you should include your PhD supervisor (or at least one of them if there is more than one). A failure to include the supervisor will certainly raise doubts in the mind of the appointing panel, and he or she will be able to comment on any teaching or other contributions that you have made to the department. If you are already in a post, then you should include someone from the department where you are working, most usually the head of department or, in a large department, the deputy chair or head of a research group. Once again, omission of someone from the department where you are working will raise doubts in the mind of the selection panel. Some applicants include the external examiner for a PhD, particularly if he or she is a prominent person in the discipline. Indeed, this may affect the choice of examiner. However, there are limits to what an external examiner can say if the viva was the only occasion when he or she met the applicant. A reference that says in essence 'X produced a good PhD that was well defended in the viva and is worthy of publication' does not add much to the information on the CV. Much the same applies to some 'great name' you have met at a conference where you gave a paper. The best references are written by the people who know you and your work well, even if they are not exalted in their status.

▶ How departments make appointments

Although the process of reducing applications to a short list can vary from department to department, and even within a department for different jobs depending in part on the urgency of the appointment, a not unusual procedure is for the departmental members of the panel to produce a long short list from the applications, for which references are then sought. Human resource departments will have required the appointing department to specify the qualities that are sought, and the skills required from the successful candidate. The appointing department may need to demonstrate that it has taken these into account in its decisions by ticking boxes. This mechanism is designed to prevent inappropriate discrimination and to provide a defence against litigation. However, departments are still principally going to be concerned in a lecturing appointment with the research record and teaching skills of the candidates. Even so, departments are not going to be enthusiastic about appointing a candidate who seems likely to cause difficulties in relations with colleagues.

It is not unusual for all the references not to have been received by the time the appointing committee meets, or for some to have arrived at the last moment. This in itself limits their value, although it is usually the case that an appointment cannot be made until all the references have been received. Given that there may be a number of candidates with uniformly enthusiastic references, it is often difficult to differentiate between them on this basis, although sometimes references can help to underline particular strengths of the candidate. What will have an impact is a 'killer' reference that either says that the candidate is not qualified for the post or damns the candidate with faint praise. If the reference is simply an attempt to demolish the candidate, it will often be set aside as inadmissible. What is really damaging is the reference that gives some grudging praise to the candidate, but then dwells at some length on various weaknesses.

If the referee has identified some pertinent weaknesses, it is unlikely that the candidate will be appointed. Some referees would tell the candidate if they felt that they could not support them, but not all do, either because they feel nervous about telling the candidate this or because they feel that they have a professional obligation to write a balanced reference that covers both strengths and weaknesses (although some referees write in such deep code that the intended message is lost). Clearly one should avoid referees whose support is qualified, but it is not always easy to identify them in advance.

▶ The interview

It is important that you prepare for the day by finding out as much as you can about the department. In addition to the information sent out with the job application forms, you should familiarize yourself with the websites of the department and the university, particularly noting any closely related departments or research centres that may be represented at the interview. It may also be useful to look at the submission for the last RAE, which is available online (www.hero.ac.uk/rae/Results/). As Luke put it, 'Find out what they're up to, find out how you fit in, make it clear that you're going to be somebody who contributes to what the department is trying to do.' Good advice 'to people going off to any sort of interview is to *be yourself*. It's counterproductive to try and shape what you say and how you present yourself to what you think the other people might want to hear' (Goldsmith, Komlos and Gold, 2001, p. 92). Maintaining a false image of yourself is psychologically wearing and ultimately unlikely to impress anyone.

Body image and self-presentation are important and you need to think carefully about what you wear for the interview. This is not a trivial matter as 'People attribute all sorts of personality characteristics to one's clothing' (Goldsmith, Komlos and Gold, 2001, p. 93). Many academics make it a point of pride to dress as scruffily as they can, apparently wearing sale items from a downmarket factory outlet. As Susan Basnett has observed (2004b, p. 54), 'it is increasingly anomalous, in a society where style and image have come to matter a great deal, that one group of professionals should be so complacent about what they look like'. Academics' seriousness sometimes seems to be judged as inversely correlated with the casualness of their dress. Basnett (2004b, p. 54) has claimed that there is a broader explanation:

> Dressing scruffily and claiming that appearances don't matter is a classic British phenomenon, part of the complex game of sending class signals to people held to be inferior. By turning up in jeans to a PhD viva, an examiner is sending a signal that says: 'Look how superior I am. I don't need to conform to any social dress codes. I am so intelligent. I am above that.'

However casual their own dress is, academics will not object if a man turns up in a suit for an interview as it seen as an appropriate uniform for the occasion. Be sure, however, that you feel comfortable in a suit. 'Wear something that you're comfortable with as being "you"; otherwise, your physical discomfort in the costume will probably be projected' (Goldsmith, Komlos and Gold, 2001, p. 92). A combination of a subtle sports jacket, neat shirt, tie and trousers with a crease is quite acceptable for men. The choice for women is more difficult. 'For women, there's no uniform, and since women are more likely to be judged on their clothing (no difference from the non-academic world here), there's greater risk in what you do wear' (Goldsmith, Komlos and Gold, 2001, p. 93). Clothes that would be perfectly suitable for a night out, such as split skirts, are not appropriate. 'Don't wear a low-cut top or a very short skirt – you want the interviewers looking at your face, not your cleavage or your legs' (Goldsmith, Komlos and Gold, 2001, p. 93). Whatever is chosen, a woman needs to be as comfortable in it sitting as well as standing. Susan Basnett (2004b) has a couple of suggestions. She refers approvingly to one woman who sat, 'in a smart, just-above-the-knee skirt and tailored over-blouse, looking thoroughly well groomed and professional' while 'One famous female academic wears only grey, but it is always well-cut grey and set off with low-key accessories, so she looks like someone to be taken seriously.' It is worthwhile discussing what you intend to wear with both your friends and with more senior women academics.

Many departments now precede the interview with a series of presentations in which candidates are invited to talk about their research or their teaching and answer questions from the audience. Normally, all members of the department are able to attend these sessions, along with colleagues from related departments or research centres. The views of these meetings are usually fed back to the appointing panel, although they often confirm or reinforce its decision rather than alter it. Strong departmental opposition to a particular candidate might, however, weigh with the panel. The panel members will also usually be present and they are likely to be influenced by the standard of the presentation. It is important to time your material so that you can deliver your key points within what is usually a limited period of between ten and 20 minutes, plus time for questions. Lauren emphasized, 'It's important to think about the way that you present, how you speak, if you keep your coat on and hunch over a desk, it's going to be less appealing.' Body language is important and you need to speak clearly and avoid mumbling, which is helped by standing up when addressing the audience.

You may also be given an opportunity to meet informally on a one-to-one basis with members of the department. Although this is a chance to learn more about the department, it may also be quite intimidating for candidates who may feel that they are being subjected to a succession of individual interviews. Sometimes departments assign a younger member of staff to show a particular candidate around and take him or her for lunch. This is not always possible, however, and sometimes applicants are taken to lunch as a group. This can be quite awkward, although it does give the applicants a chance to size up the opposition.

The interview panel may vary considerably in size and composition. The chair may be from the department or from another department, but there is usually one representative from outside the department. Good practice requires that the panel should not be composed of one gender. Although the panel might include as few as three people or more than a dozen, somewhere from six to eight would be more usual for relatively junior appointments. Not all of these may ask questions. Interview lengths vary, but for relatively junior appointments, between 20 and 30 minutes would be usual. It is as well to bear in mind 'that among the people who are interviewing you there may be deep personal or political divides. If you feel hostility during the interview it may be because of this rather than because of anything you have said' (Goldsmith, Komlos and Gold, 2001, p. 93). A number of our respondents thought that posts go to predetermined candidates, with the selection process being a means of legitimizing the preferred outcome, but you cannot be sure that is the case in relation to any given appointment, and an excellent interview could still change minds or make you a favoured candidate for a subsequent post.

There are different ways of approaching an interview, and to some extent the style you adopt will be influenced by your own personality. You have to present yourself in a way that you are comfortable with. Any attempt to present a false image will not work and will be self-defeating. You should think of questions that you may be asked and how you would answer them. Luke advised:

> Another thing I find about sitting on interview panels is how incredibly ineptly some people answer questions, particularly about teaching. A very common question is, 'You're teaching a seminar on X to 18 MA students, what are you going to do?' Answers like, 'I'm going to sit around and sort of ask what they think about X', which I've heard on many occasions, aren't going to cut it.

However much you rehearse possible answers to questions, you will never anticipate everything that may be asked. Over preparation may lead you to trot out stock answers triggered by some keyword or phrase that do not actually address the question asked. It is very difficult to deal with 'spoiling' questions, which should never be asked in the first place and whose use should be stopped by panel members from outside the department, but they are not unknown. Mike recalled that at one interview, 'I was asked an extremely aggressive question by the head of department where I could only respond by saying "I think you are wrong." That threw me.'

The chair may give you the chance to make an opening statement by asking you why you think that you are qualified for the job and what particular skills and expertise you would bring to it. Your answer should not be too long and, while you should avoid exceptional brevity, you should also avoid over-long answers throughout the interview. The longer you continue speaking, the greater the chance that you will wander off the point and start to dig a hole for yourself. The panel members may think that you are verbose and unable to explain yourself succinctly, and may start to be irritated by the fact that they might not have time to ask their questions. If you are surprised by a question, Amy advised, 'if you get a question that you can't really answer, you want to deflect it, say a little bit about it but you take control. The applicant needs to take control of the interview as much as possible.' This has to be done subtly, without seeming to be too assertive.

Unless you are being interviewed for a teaching fellowship or the department is not involved in research, you are bound to be asked about your research in the interview. Eadie notes (2005, p. 10):

> No matter what the actual job advertised states in terms of subject area or experience, the bottom line is RAE credibility. Staff quite simply must come up with the research and publication goods.

It is important not to oversell yourself, not to overstate the extent of progress on a book or to present a research agenda that is implausibly ambitious. If you are being interviewed for a contract research post, it is important that you demonstrate enthusiasm for the research being undertaken, but try to avoid suggesting that you have your own agenda that you want to reverse into the project. Contract researchers are junior members of the team and they are expected to carry out their defined duties in a conscientious and reliable way, not to attempt to take over the running of the project.

You will usually be asked at the end of the interview if there is anything you want to ask the panel. There is no obligation to ask a question at all and the panel may be relieved if you don't as they are probably running to a very tight timetable and may already be behind schedule. Detailed aspects of the job can be dealt with if and when you are made an offer. However, some candidates seem to feel it is necessary to ask questions to demonstrate their level of interest and commitment. Members of a panel are likely to groan inwardly when a candidate pulls out a long list of prepared questions. It suggests that he or she either has not researched the job well enough or is a fussy individual who is always likely to be concerned about details. Above all, do not ask odd questions. If, for example, you ask whether the university has a private dental scheme, you may offend some members of the panel who are opposed to private medicine, while others might start to wonder if there is something seriously wrong with your teeth.

Everything in this section so far has been based on the assumption that you have been interviewed in person. Occasionally, interviews relating to posts a long way from where you are may be held by videoconference or over the telephone, for example, if you or the post are in Australia. This will mean that the interview may be held at an unusual time of the day. For both the interviewers and the interviewee, a videoconference interview is not dramatically different from a face-to-face interview, except that there is usually no opportunity for presentations or any chance to meet the department. However, they are relatively expensive and therefore may not be used for relatively junior appointments. Telephone interviews are a more difficult format, even if arrangements are made so that the phone does not have to be handed from one person to the next. The fact that you are being interviewed over the telephone or by videoconference would suggest that the recruiting department is seriously interested in you.

▶ The appointment

Many universities contact candidates, most commonly by phone, as soon as possible to let them know the outcome of the interview. A widely used practice is to follow the convention of dividing candidates into 'appointable' or 'not appointable'. Candidates who are not appointable can be told the outcome very quickly. It may be necessary to keep the appointable candidates who have not been selected on hold in case the first preference candidate decides not to accept. It is not very pleasant being kept waiting in the knowledge (even if not made explicit) that you are waiting for a decision from the preferred candidate. However, if he or she declines, people will soon forget that you were the second or third-choice candidate, and you will have a job.

If you are offered the post, you should take the opportunity to discuss the details of the appointment before accepting. Obviously a new or relatively new entrant is not in the position of a 'star' professor whom the university wants to employ and can negotiate about salary, teaching hours, the recruitment of supporting lecturers or research assistants, research expenses, and so on. Nevertheless, if the employing university is really keen to recruit you, there may be some room for negotiation on salary, although you have to be very careful about how you handle this. What is important is to check out all the details of the appointment. For example, probationary staff are very often given a reduced teaching load, but you need to be clear how this is arranged and how long it lasts for. If you are required to study for a teaching certificate, you need to be sure how much time this will take and if there is a deadline for completion. If completing your PhD within a particular time period is a condition of appointment, you need to know what will happen if you miss the deadline by a few months.

You also need to find out when your office will be ready. You can be delayed while other staff move out, and this can be very frustrating at the start of a new appointment. You need to make sure that your information technology requirements are clearly understood and that there is an agreement if you need to purchase additional library books or journals (more difficult as it represents a substantial ongoing commitment) for your teaching. Above all, you need to know as soon as possible which modules you will be teaching and to talk to the module convenor if you are one of a team of teachers. It is better to sort out as many of these things as you can before you accept the appointment, as it will be more difficult later. Departments will usually be prepared to show some flexibility because they do not want to lose their chosen candidate, but there are limits to how far they can go. Requests to defer the starting date so that you can take up a visiting fellowship, for example, can be difficult in the sense that the department may have to undertake the work of making a temporary appointment to cover the teaching you would have done. Above all, bear in mind the following advice:

> It is important that you do not conflate negotiations with demands. You should not have any demands at the starting level. But the art of negotiating is really finding out what the possibilities are: what is within reach, and what is not.
>
> (Goldsmith, Komlos and Gold, 2001, p. 119)

▶ Dealing with rejection

All of us have to face failure at some point in our lives. A relationship may fail, a friendship may end, a sporting team we play for or support may fail to win a key competition. We all have different ways of coping with setbacks. Some of us may go out for (several) drinks with friends, others may take the healthier option of a thorough workout at the gym or a long run. In general, however, resilience is a valuable psychological quality that is worth developing. 'Resilience is a characteristic that lies dormant during good times, perhaps leaving that person indistinguishable from anyone else, but which becomes apparent once adversity strikes' (Persaud, 2001, p. 424). It is a difficult concept to define and there is some disagreement among psychologists about whether it is largely inherited or can be developed. In colloquial terms it means 'bouncebackability'.

It doesn't mean that you should just shrug off a job rejection, tossing the letter away and saying 'I didn't want to go there anyway.' That is a convenient rationalization, which may help you to get over the initial disappointment and help you to move forward, but it raises the question of your judgement in applying in the first place. It also does not help you to learn from the experience. It may be simply that there was a favoured internal candidate, in which case your potential learning is limited to areas like your interview technique. It may be that the prospective employers and you came to a mutual realization that you were not the right person for the job, in which case you have learnt something about the kind of job you should be applying for. It may be, however, that the interview process revealed defects in your presentation or interview technique that can be rectified. Shortcomings in what you have achieved cannot be remedied so quickly, but you may, for example, need to give priority to resubmitting an article that has been the subject of a revise and resubmit decision.

Candidates are often disappointed with the quality of the feedback they get from prospective employers. What is said in any phone call, if one is received at all, is often at the level of pleasant generalities. It is a difficult situation for whoever is making the call, as essentially he or she has to tell you that someone else was preferred. That does not mean that the person was judged to be 'better' than you, simply that he or she was more suitable for the particular post. It is probably not a good idea to ring up the department and ask for feedback if you don't receive any or to ask for more feedback if you are dissatisfied. The department may then become concerned that you are about to make a complaint about the appointing procedure and become wary in its responses. This is unfortunate for applicants, but it reflects a cautious response to a society that is perceived to be increasingly litigious. Although it is hard, try to see things from the employer's point of view. They need to recruit someone who meets their needs, not satisfy your needs.

Relatively few of us receive the job we wanted on our first application. Try to see the sequence of applications and interviews as a learning process that will help you to develop. Sooner or later you will receive an offer. If, however, you persistently fail even to be interviewed, or you are repeatedly interviewed, but fail to secure a post, you may need to consider other career options such as academic administration. Adjusting your expectations in this way is not easy, but you may ultimately have a more successful career. A colleague discovered early in his career that he lacked talent as a researcher, switched to university administration and eventually occupied a sequence of increasingly senior positions, first in individual universities and then in the university system as a whole. If he had stayed as a lecturer, he would have failed to progress.

Alternative careers

If a PhD fails to lead to a permanent academic appointment, this does not mean that it has been a waste of time. Apart from those PhDs who decided to pursue a career in a university, research council or other academic administration, where the experience of having completed a PhD is seen as relevant and valuable, there are many other career opportunities open to PhDs. For example, within the field of political science and international relations, they can be found working in government, the European Commission or international organizations, trade associations, government relations divisions of companies or even as ministers. Business school PhDs are often employed by companies or work as consultants. Humanities PhDs may work for publishers, literary journals, foundations, archives, galleries or museums. Skills developed in the PhD can be deployed in these settings and new skills acquired that may eventually lead to the resumption of an academic career that is then more psychologically and materially rewarding than it would have been if a more conventional route had been followed. If nothing else, a period outside academic life may lead to a greater appreciation of its special advantages. Contemporary postgraduates follow a more flexible career path, and using their intelligence and skills in the academic sector is not the only or best way forward. Critical analytical skills can be valuable in a wide variety of settings in the public and private sectors, and being an intellectual in such a context may bring its own special rewards.

Nevertheless, this book is constructed on the assumption that the reader wants to follow an academic career and will eventually succeed in obtaining a full-time appointment, even though other career routes may be equally valid and rewarding. Once you have obtained a post, how can you be successful in it? This forms the theme of the next chapter.

3 Managing Your Work

Once you have secured your job, you want to be a success in it. The transition from being a doctoral student and a part-time teacher to a full-time member of staff can be a greater shock than you anticipated. Maria, an older new entrant with children, found it 'overwhelming'. Ian commented:

> I underestimated entirely what the transition from being an associate to a full-time member of staff would be. I suspected that I would teach less and be paid more. While those things are true, I also do a lot more administration and I also have much more responsibility for the units I teach.

'Success' means different things for different people. Without having too rigid a plan, it is helpful to have some idea of what you want to achieve and how you might achieve it. As Luke put it:

> Have a sense of what you want to achieve, try and set yourself goals, try to be aware of what are the most effective ways to do that and often the answer is the same, at one level to become a good citizen of your department, you have plenty of examples of academic careers that are long in the tooth but short on promotion. In some senses that doesn't necessarily boil down to incompetence, it boils down to lack of savvy, not understanding there are various ways in which you can make a contribution.

Academic careers can follow many different routes, each of which can bring different forms of success. As Lauren observed:

> There are all sorts of different profiles that one can achieve in academia. One can have a profile as someone who brings in lots of money but not having a particularly high scholarly reputation. One can have a profile as a wheeler and dealer and as a mover and shaker. One can have a very high scholarly reputation but no one knows who you are. The first thing is to decide what sort of profile you want to have.

What sort of profile is appropriate in the early stage of an academic career? The choices you make will be conditioned to some extent by the institution and the department you are working in and its expectations, and also by your own goals. 'Success' is not just about external forms of recognition such as promotion. These are important, but in a career which has strong vocational elements to it you need to be at peace with yourself in the sense of maintaining your own integrity by working in a way that you think is worthwhile and achieving broader objectives. That in itself will help to bring satisfaction and contentment. However, more instrumental considerations cannot be disregarded. For most young academics, bringing in large sums in grant money or establishing a reputation as a mover and shaker will have to wait until a later stage in their career, if that is what they want.

Success in the early stage of your career is going to be largely governed by your performance in teaching and research. You also need to be a competent administrator, but, as is emphasized later, this should be done in a way that does not distract you too much from your two core tasks. Being seen as a conscientious, well-organized and inspirational teacher will enhance your departmental reputation, although perhaps more with students than with other staff members, despite the importance of questionnaires and other feedback mechanisms. It can also be a source of great satisfaction and feed into your research, particularly if you are open to learning from students. However, unless you win a prize for outstanding teaching, it is unlikely to have much effect on your external reputation.

▶ Raising your academic profile

In the early stage of your career you need to establish your reputation in your discipline through publication (dealt with in Chapter 6), attendance and participation at conferences and other activities. The importance of publication in raising a profile cannot be emphasized too strongly. It is a key means of getting yourself known as someone who has something distinctive and interesting to say. If it is a good one, the publication will be in use for a number of years and hence will serve as a constant reminder to others of your interests and contribution. Good work speaks for itself and a reputation for work of high quality that moves forward debates in your discipline will give you the best possible profile.

Conferences

Conferences are a key part of making oneself known and developing networks. Ruth commented:

> Conferences are useful for networking. They are useful for showcasing a particular piece of work. They are important in the sense that so much of a person's academic career depends upon who they know rather than what they know, and being in the right time in the right place with the right person. This has occurred to me over a number of years – and in particular 'bar' time – the informal time outside the formal sessions.

Not everyone enjoys networking, and while this book was being written, an otherwise very successful young academic whose practice was to shut herself in her room and work when formal sessions were not taking place was persuaded to come to the bar at a conference. She found the informal interaction invaluable for her work. You are not obliged to drink alcohol, and there are other opportunities for informal interaction over coffee. It is here that you can meet publishers and journal editors who may be interested in your work. Publishers often have their own receptions and appointments can be made to meet commissioning editors, but this should be done in advance as they have busy schedules.

Conferences come in many shapes and sizes and there are some variations by disciplines. But broadly speaking four types can be recognized:

1. Major international conferences, often held in the United States with several thousand delegates and meetings spread over several hotels in a big city.
2. The national conference held by a disciplinary association.
3. More specialist conferences held by sub-disciplinary groupings, often affiliated to the disciplinary association.
4. Specialist workshops on a particular topic with participation limited to those who are invited.

Finding one's way around a major international conference can be a daunting experience even for senior academics as, still jet lagged, you queue for the elevator, wait for the shuttle bus to another hotel or try to locate the panel you want to attend. It is no accident that conferences form a recurrent theme in academic novels. Nevertheless, Luke emphasized:

I found being active in international conferences incredibly useful, you just encounter people, particularly in the States, who would otherwise have no particular reason to encounter you. I think that the primary function of international conferences is less the intellectual exchange but the fact that you make connections with people.

Attending an international conference needs planning several months in advance, particularly if you want to present a paper. Indeed, presenting a paper is often necessary to unlock travel funds from your department or external sources. Despite their large scale, panel slots at such conferences are generally highly competitive and prior contacts with someone organizing a panel or a segment of the programme can be helpful. If you can afford to do so, it is worth staying at one of the conference hotels, which usually discount their normal prices. Staying some way away in cheaper accommodation can limit your opportunities to take advantage of the informal opportunities for interaction that the conference provides. If the conference is being held in a time zone that is substantially different from the UK, it is often worth arriving at least 24 hours in advance of the start of the conference. This will enable you to get over the worst of your jet lag and to become familiar with the layout of the conference venue. You could even consider taking a short holiday in the location before the conference starts. Don't dismiss any sightseeing trips provided by the conference organizers as distractions from your main task. They may provide excellent opportunities to talk informally to other delegates, including senior members of your discipline.

Organizers of national disciplinary association conferences face something of a dilemma. They generally want the events to be as inclusive as possible of younger scholars, but they also want to attract the 'big hitters' in the discipline. There is a tendency observable in some disciplines for the leading figures to confine themselves to major international conferences or specialist workshops with invited memberships. Indeed, such is the pressure of academic globalization that younger staff may be told to prioritize international conferences before national ones. National association conferences may have the excessive breadth of international conferences without the associated prestige. Nevertheless, they can be a valuable means of making useful contacts and getting your name more widely known. If you are in a temporary post, they may be a way of finding out about jobs that are going to be advertised and also of making yourself known to people who might hire you. Zoe found them 'particularly helpful at the beginning [of her career], especially a good way to meet people in the broader discipline as distinct from people who only do [my specialisms]'.

Sub-disciplinary conferences allow you to meet people in your particular field. They often enjoy a strong intellectual reputation and give rise to edited books (often a yearbook) or a special issue of a specialist journal. They are a good way of making yourself known in your own research niches and establishing a reputation. However, if things go wrong the consequences may be more serious than at a more general conference. Luke's first paper was 'monstered' by a leading figure in his discipline at a major conference. Although he saw it as 'an obligatory rite of passage', the consequences in terms of damage to reputation could be more serious in a specialist conference.

An invitation to a specialist workshop is a sign that you are being recognized as a contributor in your field. Often they are held in very attractive locations: Bellagio in Italy has even featured in an academic novel. Nevertheless, it can be a daunting experience to suddenly find yourself closeted for two or three days with the leaders in your field. Remember, however, that you have been invited because it is thought that you have something worthwhile to contribute. The 'big hitters' there will be secure in their reputations and most of them will not feel threatened by a younger academic. If you are not giving a formal presentation, try to intervene as soon as a sensible opportunity presents itself. It will make you less nervous and nobody will be impressed if you stay silent throughout the proceedings. Do not, however, use a technique that has been seen in operation, attacking the middle rankers in the workshop in the view that they are easier targets and the 'big hitters' might be impressed. The middle rankers may feel more need to defend themselves and may be more formidable than anticipated. They may also be 'supporting actors' of the stars, who will not be pleased about their acolytes being criticized.

There are some key points that ensure a successful conference presentation that are often neglected. Even senior academics are often bad at timing, but if you have a period of, say, 15 minutes to present, make sure that you use it effectively. Don't place yourself in a position where your key points have to be rushed through at the end or even not made at all. If there is a discussant or discussants, make sure that they have your paper well in advance. If you are going to use PowerPoint or overhead projector slides, make sure that the necessary facilities are available (surprisingly they are often not automatically available in major American hotels). Make sure that PowerPoint presentations are loaded on to the facilities being used. Delays caused by problems with the PowerPoint are an invariable feature of almost any conference. Although PowerPoint is attractive to people who find public speaking difficult, it can encourage the production of tedious lists and can be a substitute for communication rather than a means of facilitating it (Atkinson, 2004; Tufte, 2003). Nevertheless, its use is often seen as a hallmark of professionalism. Be careful, though, of letting the style of the presentation overcome the substance.

However good your slides, you will still have to speak. Positioning yourself well in relation to a microphone is not always easy and can be a further unwelcome distraction at the start of your presentation. If you speak without a microphone, try to project your voice to the back of the room. How easy this is will depend in part on how well acoustically designed the room is. Whatever you do, don't mumble and don't speak too rapidly, a natural reaction to nervousness. Don't be disappointed at a major conference if the panel is bigger than the audience. Often small audiences produce the best discussions, and the people there are likely to be the ones to invite you to offer an article based on your paper to a major refereed journal.

Professional associations

Joining your professional disciplinary association (or perhaps more than one) is a good idea if only because it usually entitles you to discounts on annual conferences and journals and access to specialist workshops. Many associations have specialist groups that relate to particular areas of the discipline and you should certainly get involved in any group relevant to your interests, perhaps offering to organize a workshop. Some associations have funds available to help younger staff members to attend conferences or even travel abroad. Involvement beyond membership can be a good way of raising your profile. Taking on some mundane task within your association will earn you the gratitude of your more senior colleagues. They will also be receptive to ideas from younger members of the discipline about specialist workshops or conference panels as they will want to respond to new ideas and trends within the discipline. As Luke observed:

> Finding some kind of broader citizenship role is quite useful. In some senses your intellectual qualities are taken for granted as being things that define how good you are but in addition to that I think if you just plough your furrow and don't push yourself out into the broader disciplinary universe you probably won't get the recognition that you probably deserve.

Zoe followed a deliberate strategy of seeking election to executive committees, first of her sub-disciplinary association and then to her disciplinary association. Do not assume that such committee positions are reserved for senior members of the profession. Professional associations will want to represent the diversity of their membership on their executive committees so the fact that you are, for example, at a post-1992 university is an asset rather than a disqualification. In Zoe's case, the contribution she made was recognized by her being made a member of a small search committee set up to choose the next chair of the association.

What you should avoid if at all possible is being the local organizer for a major conference (as distinct from a specialist workshop). Departments will too often 'volunteer' a young member of staff for this task. Even with clerical support and postgraduate 'gofers', it can be a nightmare. Academics often have great difficulty in stipulating their requirements precisely and then want to change them at the last minute.

You may find yourself dealing in the small hours of the morning with delegates who are inebriated and cannot find or have locked themselves out of their rooms. Woe betide you if anyone gets left behind on the coach trip to a local attraction. If the conference is a success, you will be thanked by your department and the association and then everyone will start thinking about next year's event. If anything goes wrong, people will be talking about it and your part in it for years afterwards. Fortunately, associations are increasingly recognizing that they have to bring in professionals to run their conferences.

In some disciplines, there are specialized institutes that provide an important focus for academic work and were mentioned by respondents as another forum for raising their profile. For example, the Institute of Historical Research in London describes itself as the national centre for history and runs a range of conferences as well as three research centres. The Goethe Institute is important for German studies scholars and has undertaken work on such themes as church–state relations and education. The Alliance Française is the French equivalent and has a particular strength in the study of cinema. The Maison Française d'Oxford, funded by the French government, is the only European research centre of its type in the UK and gives academics the opportunity to engage in dialogue with leading French thinkers.

Media work
Our respondents were generally sceptical of the value of media work as a means of raising one's profile or of contributing to career development.

Although regret is something expressed about the lack of 'public intellectuals', such individuals are often regarded with a mixture of envy and scepticism in their own disciplines. You have to consider who is going to benefit from a media interview. Journalists often already know the story they want to write and need a quote to support it or they will pump you for background information that will be used in the story with no reference to you. Institutions usually encourage media work as it raises their profile, both in the local community and more widely, but their interest is in the benefit to the institution rather than you. Press officers may exaggerate your expertise in a particular area or encourage you to make appearances that will do your reputation no good. Media work is unlikely to be a decisive factor in promotion decisions.

Lucy took the view that it could actually damage a career if taken too far:

> I think that actually it's all a bit dubious, I think there is a kind of new trend of media don and I think that there is a probably a lot of resentment against those people either through jealousy or because other people want to do it and can't. But I also think that if you spend that much time in the media perhaps you are neglecting other things in academia. I don't really think this new kind of trend is that good.

It might be argued, and certainly would be argued by research councils, that academics have a responsibility to disseminate their findings to a wider audience.

It is also a means of demonstrating to a wider public that the university education they help to fund has a wider relevance. For most academics, particularly younger ones, the programmes they are likely to be invited on to will often have small audiences and the questions they will be asked will test their expertise, but not in a particularly academically demanding way. To take three examples from Wyn Grant's experience, he has been asked to:

- explain the significance of the American presidential election result for a particular locality on a local radio station
- explain on daytime television to a young girl why her pony cannot contract BSE
- talk about 'Englishness' on live television in front of Shakespeare's birthplace.

The media themselves can be very demanding of your time and expect you to drop everything while you talk to them. Do not be surprised if you are rung early in the morning for an interview or asked to stand by at such an hour and then dropped from the programme when someone more important becomes available. One appearance may, however, lead to another, as the media is quite incestuous in the way that it develops stories. For example, Wyn Grant was interviewed by Radio 5 in the early morning, a television crew was sent to his home mid-morning and he was then invited on to live television at lunchtime.

If you do intend to do a lot of media work, it is best to take a training course of the kind offered by research councils or some professional associations. You will then master the basics of what to wear on television and how to avoid 'dead air' (silence) or a 'dropped bird' (talking over a jingle) on radio. You may come to enjoy doing the late shift on a radio phone-in when there are only three callers waiting and it is likely that they are either inebriated or deranged or both. However, see it as an enjoyable distraction from your usual work, rather than a key step in career development.

▶ Time management

As an academic you will never have enough time to do everything that you want to do. It therefore seems sensible to think about how you can make effective use of the finite time available to you. However, apart from suggestions such as setting aside research days, our interview respondents had very few suggestions to offer on time management and some confessed that they were not very good at it. Lauren noted that, 'Academics tend not to be very well organized!' This might reflect less a tendency of the profession to attract people who are not well organized, than certain inherent tensions within it. Academics are affected not only by the pressures of an increasingly demanding external environment, but also by internal pressures arising from standards of excellence that they set themselves. There is a tendency for new entrants to set themselves very high standards that cannot be easily achieved. The standard advice in many general time management manuals (a web search yielded over 2500 books with over 200 directed specifically at undergraduates) to only do things 'well enough' may not be heeded. Academics are maximizers rather than satisficers. One of the hardest lessons for a new academic to learn is that one doesn't always have to be a perfectionist. As Ian commented, 'It's a very useful skill to know how and when to cut corners.' Remember the 80:20 rule originally devised by the economist Pareto which states that 80 per cent of the reward comes from 20 per cent of the effort. Of course, to make use of this you need to know which 20 per cent of the effort pays off, and some hints on this will be given below.

It has to be recognized that academic life does make considerable time demands on its practitioners and for that reason it may not be the most suitable career for some people. Ian enjoyed the challenge of combining different types of task: 'The marvellous thing for me is the flexibility and the fact that it is tremendously varied. Be aware of whether you're the kind of person that enjoys the challenge of balancing a few things.' Ruth said that she had actively sought a non-academic job: 'The principal reason is to get my weekends and evenings back, and one of the really attractive things for me about going into the civil service is the idea that you can get in at 9 or 10 am and go home at 4 or 5.' The grass may always look greener on the other side, however. Globalization is a highly contested concept, but one of the consequences of intensified international competition, extending into what were formerly protected public services, is time pressure in all managerial and professional jobs, reflected in a 'long hours' culture where you are not seen as doing the job properly if you are not working late. At least academics have the option of working from home for some of the time.

Lucy pointed out that the very nature of academic life made it difficult to clearly differentiate work and leisure:

> I actually find the 'treat academia as a 9 to 5 job' difficult. In English you're thinking all the time. I think I spend more time working [than on leisure] but I've made the choice and I think that because I still see academia as a vocation I think that people who complain how much work they have to do should go and do a job where their hours are more clearly demarcated rather than saying academia should change.

Realistically academics have to expect to work quite long hours in the early phases of their careers when they are building their research and teaching portfolios. Although saying 'no' to particular requests is a skill that has to be learnt, Lucy noted, 'I think that it is good at the start to just try and do as much as possible and to know the community within your field.' If, for example, you turn down a request to write a book review, you are unlikely to be asked by that particular journal again.

There are certain key rights that we need to protect, however great our dedication to our academic discipline as a vocation (see Box 3.1). As Luke put it, 'The key is creating clear boundaries, drawing up a personal contract with yourself to make certain kinds of tasks non-negotiable.' As Amy noted:

> I think there comes a point when people hit a point and they say, 'I cannot work flat out any more.' I hit that point, my husband hit that point, we just had an academic friend come over from the US last weekend and she said, 'How can you have a family? And commute? And research? And teach? And do administration?' And she said, 'I'm just working all the time.' And I said you just hit a point where you say 'enough is enough'.

However, there are limits to how far this can be taken. As Lewis and Hills (1999, pp. 107–8) warn, 'We assume that when saying "no" threatens our continued employment, this form of time protection is becoming altogether too costly.' Refusing to do something can have adverse consequences, but this has to be balanced against the consequences of never saying no. Achieving a work–life balance is not easy for academics, although they are not alone in facing such problems. As Luke explained, 'The problem with academic work is there's never closure. It's a peculiar problem of academic life, it does tend to colonise you. I just now refuse to work on Saturdays.' Other respondents said that they tried to keep one day clear at the weekends, often under pressure from their partners and families. Lauren said that she had to have a conversation with herself to maintain a work–life balance, although she thought it would be easier for someone who had children, as then there would be certain things you would be compelled to do. If you are concerned about your work–life balance, you might be interested in the

---

Box 3.1 The outer limits of acceptable workload

- Each of us is subject to a personal upper limit beyond which any attempt to do more will be counter-productive, because beyond this point, our total 'output' will actually drop.
- We have a right to a private life, to a family life, to some waking time on personal projects.
- We have a right to health – and so a right to contain the demands (and stresses) of work so that our health is not threatened.

Source: Lewis and Hills (1999), p. 109.

online quiz provided by the Mental Health Foundation at http://www.mhtn.org/quiz.

Some advice on time management

There is a sense in which 'Time is not a dimension that, as such, cannot be influenced or "managed"' (Lewis and Hills, 1999, p. 2). Although it can be quantified like money, it is much more difficult to estimate how long it will take us to write an article compared with how much a replacement car might cost. Time management is really 'a mode of "self-management". To get time under control there are no magic tricks, only a small number of techniques which help us to form good habits of time management' (Lewis and Hills, 1999, p. 19). The particular techniques we deploy depend on our own personal preferences. A 'one size fits all' approach does not work. What you need to do is to work out for yourself the rules and procedures that suit you best and to do this you require to be 'metacognitive' about time. In other words, you need to recognize that 'time management' is something you have to think about systematically. Checking where your time is being wasted is a good exercise for us all.

The difficulty of giving advice that is generally applicable is reflected in two sets of differences between academics that emphasize the importance of asking yourself the right questions about the type of person you are and how you work best. First, because of differences in our body clocks some of us are good at working early in the day, while others can work late at night. It is good practice to think about your own biological prime time. Are you a 'morning person' or a 'night owl'? Some of us like to deal with emails as a first task of the day as a means of 'warming up'. Others deal them with in odd portions of time throughout the day or prefer to leave them to the end of the day when they are less energetic and less able to do creative work. Secondly, some (relatively few) academics have neat and tidy offices with everything in its place; others have offices that are apparently chaotic in which they are nevertheless able to find what they want with ease because for them disorder is a form of organization. One should not push this too far, however. Simple organizational systems using filing cabinets can save much time, particularly on administrative tasks. Ian pointed to his untidy office, but said that he operated a 'clean desk' policy so that everything would be put back in place at the end of the day. If you can't do this once a day, at least tidy your office once a week.

If you do not deploy any time management techniques, you will not be able to use the scare resource of time in such a way that you work effectively. You will be constantly overwhelmed by the pressure of unfinished tasks. When this happens, it is likely that it is your research and writing rather than your other activities that suffer. Lectures have to be given at a time arranged in advance; exam scripts have to be marked by a deadline. Most academics find they need considerable periods of time set aside to write effectively. It is not something that can be picked up for an hour and then put down again. As Lauren commented, 'I need a run-up and some time to get into my stride and stay there for a bit.'

A number of respondents drew attention to the importance of vacations as a time when it was possible to progress one's research. Luke noted, 'Breaks, vacations are a deeply precious commodity when it comes to sitting down and actually thinking and writing.' One helpful technique may be to plan how you use this time and set yourself targets that are demanding but feasible. These targets should reflect the *effective* use of time rather than earmarking particular quantities of time when you expect to work. In other words, you need to consider what is the right thing to do before thinking about how to do it.

Academic work, particularly writing, is a highly creative task and it cannot be turned on and off like a tap. Our ability to write may be subtly affected by our mood. There may be days when it is just necessary to recognize that the work isn't going to flow. The best thing may be then to take a complete break and go to the gym, take a swim, do some gardening, play a musical instrument or whatever activity you find relaxing. Don't feel guilty about taking a refreshing break. Good ideas may come to you while you are undertaking a physically demanding or mundane task.

A number of respondents emphasized that the key to effective time management was self-discipline, but some people are better at that than others. Making 'to do' lists of outstanding work is a very simple technique that can be very effective, but it also brings to the surface a tension between rigidity and flexibility. Establishing a routine also requires sufficient flexibility to abandon that routine when unexpected circumstances make it advantageous to do so. Making 'to do' lists can often become an excuse for delaying starting work. Target setting can be demotivating when obstacles delay (as they will). Prioritizing tends to give precedence to urgent tasks as distinct from important long-term tasks such as keeping up with the journals. Craig summarized the dilemma:

> There are pluses and minuses to being immensely disciplined with your time. In periods of starting a new job, whether it's your first job or you've had a job previously, the first year is always a nightmare. The only way of doing it is to be immensely disciplined, setting yourself short-term targets, hitting those targets, but then things always come along to interfere with those targets.

For all the drawbacks of 'to do' lists, there is some value in having an idea of what needs to be done in a particular day or week, alongside a general set of research targets for the academic year. When you are making long-term plans for research projects, remember to allocate sufficient time to the different phases of the project. A common error is to allow too much time for research design and planning, start field work too soon and leave insufficient time for writing up. Once you have 'to do' lists, one strategy is to focus first on a number of tasks that are likely to take up less time, but would cause problems if they were not tackled quickly. Simply getting these tasks out of the way can give more satisfaction. However, there is a risk that 'doing the easy things first' may not leave enough time for the hard work. The actual order in which different types of work is tackled should reflect your personal habits and preferences. Set yourself objectives that are realistic and achievable but do stretch you to some extent so that achieving them will represent real progress on outstanding tasks.

One technique that some people find useful, to complement setting time aside for major tasks like writing, is to earmark a day as a 'clearing the decks' day. This is a day when one attempts to clear a series of relatively minor tasks that require attention. As Lauren put it,

> I find it helps to have a concerted push at clearing the mountain of things that are always sitting waiting for attention, and spending a full day or two on it tends not only to make inroads but make me feel a bit more like I'm on top of things.

You will also be free of nagging worry about uncompleted minor tasks when you concentrate on your research and writing. However, don't let this develop into a situation where you are always completing minor tasks but never tackling major ones.

Working at home

Our respondents were in general agreement that they liked to do their more creative work at home rather than in the office. Ian emphasized that his office at home was key to a strategy in which 'I try to make myself some physical and temporal space. That space is essential to get into the right mind set.' Luke amplified the advantages of working from home:

> Two at home, three in office average week. I like to think that even if I was five minutes away, I'd be doing the same. The reason for that is although I work well in the office, there I tend to find there's lots of passing traffic and there's lots of things on my desk. This is one of the ways of drawing a boundary, to physically

relocate yourself where you've only got materials relating to whatever it is you're writing. So that's what you're doing rather than having a pile of memos, which are demanding things that you get on with straight away. By and large I find that if I come in here on a term time weekday and I don't have any obvious commitments then I will be sucked into the administrative side of things.

Lauren, however, cautioned against spending too much time working at home: 'There's a strong case for making sure you're seen in the office, there are people who are hardly ever seen in the office.' However, if you are around in the office frequently, you may get allocated tasks simply because you are there. Being present may get you credit as a good departmental citizen, but do little for your longer-term career. If you have to come into the office a lot because of your teaching and administrative responsibilities, think about how you organize your time there so that it is not frittered away. Zoe noted,

> I have been coming in at 8 am three days a week, which gives you a chance to get your stuff done before you are bothered by students because they won't turn up before 10, that's made quite a difference.

Avoiding perfectionism in teaching

Ann put the case for being 'robustly selfish' in time management, noting that gender biases might arise if women were perceived as being better with students and at administration. It was evident from our interviews that, particularly when faced with higher loads in post-1992 universities, new entrants were being too perfectionist with their teaching, and this was not good for them or for the students. The problem was compounded in post-1992 universities by new staff being required to teach modules that had no relevance to their interests and of which they had no prior knowledge. Thus, an expert on the Holocaust might be required to teach Irish literature and an expert on the English Republic might be needed to contribute to more popular courses on the Nazis. Some members of staff were clearly overwhelmed with reading new texts.

Respondents were aware of the fact that they were over-preparing, but found it difficult to do anything about it. Ian referred to 'the dangers of being over-prepared [and] the danger of stifling discussion by having too much to say. The only way to get over that is by gradually increasing confidence which is a matter of time.' As far as lectures are concerned, remember that students (generally) know less than you, can only absorb so much learning, and that you should communicate clearly and simply. In seminars, students need to develop transferable skills of working on their own and with others and presenting their findings. Only in that way will they develop a capacity for independent thought, which requires an independence from the tutor who is there to guide and structure the discussion, not to dominate through conveying all the knowledge stocked up from over-preparation.

Craig had reflected about the challenge of stifling student learning through over-preparation and offered good advice:

> Early on in one's career it's inevitable that you over-prepare and as time goes on with experience you realize not only that that level of preparation is not always necessary and stems from a lack of confidence, but quite often that that over-preparation can strangle a class, and with that experience comes the confidence to know just how much is necessary, just where the line comes. You can close a class down by wanting to bring all that preparation to a class. You learn how to allow a class to breathe. Over-preparation can put the emphasis too much on you as the tutor, whereas at least in seminars the emphasis ought to be on guiding the students.

Coping with administrative work

There is no doubt that the intrusion into their time that was most resented by our respondents was administrative work, particularly those in older universities. In part this is because, while they were enthused by teaching and research, administration did not have the same attractions for most of them. If they had wanted to spend their time engaged in those sorts of tasks, they could have pursued a career as a university administrator, although some respondents in post-1992 universities saw a clear alternative career route in academic management. The timing of administrative work can be particularly onerous and inconvenient. 'The variety of unavoidable administrative tasks includes many that have their own urgent and short deadlines, which come at times that are unpredictable and thus highly inopportune' (Lewis and Hills, 1999, p. 60). As Luke commented, 'The [administrative] load strikes me as being heavy ... It's not about physical mass in terms of heaviness, it's about the intensity and the urgency of something and the fact that often you're committed to portions of time.' Probationary arrangements should offer new entrants some protection against onerous administrative burdens, but our interviews suggest that even in research universities they are honoured as much in the breach as in the observance. In her first post in an older university, Ann was appointed examinations secretary in a large department. Faced with the challenge of persuading senior colleagues to amend their examination papers, she noted dryly, 'It's difficult being in such a role when you're in a temporary position and 30 years younger. Mild flattery worked.'

The difficulty from the viewpoint of departmental chairs is that if someone is not doing an administrative task, it has to be assigned to someone else. There is a perception however, stated by Ruth, that 'people at the more junior end of the hierarchy get a heavier burden of administrative tasks'. What is certain is that you will be unable to avoid some administrative tasks. It is therefore important to be very clear about when you are wearing your administrator's hat and when you are not. Make sure that you have appropriate systems in place and attend to tasks such as record keeping, for example, making a note of conversations from students after they have taken place. It is important to given an impression of being well organized and being confidently in charge of things, even if you are not. If you don't know the answer to a question, try to find it out as quickly as you can. Identify administrative staff at faculty or university level who can provide you with such information and develop good relationships with them. Be familiar with how relevant information is organized on the university's Intranet so that you can access it quickly when you need it.

It is the nature of some tasks, of course, that they will peak at certain times of the year, for example, examinations secretary or admissions tutor. The burden can then to some extent be foreseen, but it may effectively prevent any other work being undertaken at the particular time. It is also important not to be too perfectionist about administrative work without neglecting it. No one is going to get promoted because he or she was an outstandingly good exams secretary. There is also the risk that if you are seen to be an efficient administrator you will be given tasks in the wider university and before you know where you are you will be deputy chair of the safety committee or put on a working party on emergency generating equipment. Equally, if you make a mess of a key administrative task, or fail to do it all, your colleagues will not forget or forgive quickly. It is also worth bearing in mind that if you have a task such as examinations secretary that brings you into contact with senior members of your discipline, discharging your duties efficiently may make a good impression on them. They may then come to see you as someone who would be a good research collaborator.

Working with support staff
Many aspects of administrative work will bring you into close and frequent contact with support staff. The day-to-day operation of a

department depends on these individuals. The role of these staff has changed over the years. There has been a move away from the model of the departmental secretary, often a mature woman, who combined her administrative duties with dispensing advice and support to students. Larger departments may now have an administrator, perhaps with accountancy qualifications, who may to some extent be seen by the central administrative services as their representative in the department. There might also be a chair's secretary and distinct graduate and undergraduate offices providing an interface with students. What should not be underestimated is the influence that support staff can have. Van der Berghe (1970, p. 34) notes:

> Secretaries are often the best informed persons about departmental affairs – amorous, political, and scholarly. They can wield considerable influence over departmental chairmen and other figures. Never presume to be of higher status than they are.

It is important to avoid friction with support staff, but also not to get drawn into taking sides in conflicts that can arise between support staff. They are often put under simultaneous pressure by students and staff, particularly at busy times of the year such as examinations. One thing they particularly dislike is not being able to contact staff when a problem arises, so let them have your mobile number and respond courteously if they contact you when you are working at home. If they have a particular way of working which you do not like or find inconvenient, for example, processing examination results, suggest any changes as tactfully as possible. Above all, do not address them in an imperious manner, issuing them with orders and instructions. Treat them as fellow team workers in the way that you would an academic colleague. Asked for just one tip she would give a new member of academic staff, Lucy responded, 'Be respectful and nice to the secretaries, because they're the people who control the department and they're the people who work the hardest.'

▶ Developing good working relationships with colleagues

Academics in the humanities and social sciences often see themselves in a very individualistic light, working almost as individual entrepreneurs, even if they do collaborate on particular projects with colleagues. In the natural sciences, the laboratory draws people together to work in teams. But in the humanities, much work is done in archives and libraries, while in the social sciences academics may pursue their own schedule of interviews or carry out their own work on a data set. These ways of working may have been reinforced by the pressures arising from the RAE. Lucy commented,

> One of the problems with academia is that there is this kind of 'shut yourself in your office and do the research so that you can get the RAE score'. If things were done more communally, if there was more emphasis on team teaching and team projects, I think we'd all be much better off really.

Referring to a department in a leading research university, Amy noted,

> I have friends who in the past have complained, 'Everybody here's just so focused and nobody lives around in the area, we never do anything social, nobody ever wants to have lunch.' At a top research university, the university is saying the government says 'research', so that's what you get rewarded for.

But as Zoe noted, 'Being friendly actually helps you get through difficult times and there have been some.'

Departments can be factionalized, and Craig reflected on the challenges this could present:

> I'm now in a situation of being a new person here where I'm just feeling my way through the politics of the particular department and there are always those political factions and undercurrents and that can be quite difficult and it can be quite daunting as well when you find yourself among some well rooted political tensions in a department between colleagues who can dislike one another quite intensely. I'm finding that I'm just keeping my head down, learning what's going on and just going about doing my job and trying not to get involved in any of that because quite often it's very petty.

Lewis and Hills (1999, p. 101) point out that 'time spent on developing good working relationships, and time spent on dealing with interpersonal difficulties or conflicts, is not necessarily time wasted, even if it is taken from our "primary" activities of teaching and research.' As they note:

> If relationships are good, then mutual support in time management is just one of the many benefits we can enjoy; and if relationships are sour, not only is effectiveness challenged, but in the worst cases all

efforts at control of time may be derailed. If we find ourselves embroiled in a feud, or if we become convinced that other colleagues are trying in some way to undermine our position, we may become so involved in dealing with the problem and in brooding about it that work on other tasks is sabotaged.

Some sensitivity and understanding of the position of others is necessary for effective working. Craig dealt with relationship problems 'by being immensely up front and just going along to that particular colleague's office and smoothing things. I feel personally able to do that, a lot of people don't and won't.' Even if you can't do that, try to avoid the 'flaming' email that can make a bad situation worse. If something that has happened that has irritated or upset you, pause for reflection for 24 hours before taking any action. Consider how important the problem will seem in a month's time or a year's time. Sometimes people simply have a bad day and they take it out on the nearest available target and it would be unfortunate if such an incident led to an ongoing deterioration in relationships. As Luke advised:

> Try to understand that when people get a bit grumpy with you they are actually not grumpy with you. Having a sense of a human being's worth, having a notion of psychology sometimes, anger and grumpiness is often transferred, it's not yours, it doesn't belong to you, you just happen to be the target at the time. Respond either by taking the wind out of their sails or, if necessary, just being robust, standing up if you think you've not made a mistake, you've behaved properly, then you make that clear.

Some of the interpersonal communication skills taught on counselling courses may be of relevance to developing better relations with colleagues, and if your university offers an introductory course in counselling it may be worth taking it. Wyn Grant took one at his university and found it a valuable investment of time, particularly in terms of developing listening skills. Of course, counselling is more than about 'just assembling a set of skills' (Sanders, 2002, p. 67), but a counselling course can be taken without the intention of becoming a counsellor. It may also help with your pastoral care of students. A core value in counselling is empathy:

> This is trying to see the world of another person from their point of view. It involves trying to understand their world, their meanings, their life. It has been described as walking in someone else's

shoes, understanding how they feel and think – listening to both the 'words' and the 'music'.

(Sanders, 2002, p. 68)

Academics are very used to being asked what they *think*, but are much less accustomed to being asked what they *feel*. This is not surprising when, particularly in the social sciences, much of their work involves making rational or rules-based judgements. Intellectualizing quickly may be easier and safer, but trying to identify and access feelings may be important in handling one's relationships with colleagues. This is not easy and it may be difficult to empathize with a colleague who is being obnoxious or difficult. Indeed, there are limits to how far one should try to understand their position, an issue returned to in the discussion of bullying and harassment later in the chapter. Academics have always been competitive to some extent, and it is tempting to believe in the myth of a golden age of collegiality when everyone sat at high table or in the senior common room discussing great ideas. Nevertheless,

> An unwelcome side effect of other changes – in resources, in pressures on departments to perform – has been an increase in conflict among colleagues … colleagues whose idiosyncratic ways seemed lovable or at the least tolerable, are now felt to be a liability.
>
> (Lewis and Hills, 1999, p. 13)

Ruth observed, 'It would be nice to think that we can all be friends and work in a cooperative environment, but my view, more and more, is that it is a competitive environment.'

While colleagues can be irritating or even obstructive, it is worth investing some effort in developing relationships with them. Setting boundaries can pose problems, but it is probably counterproductive to insist on too rigid a distinction between the personal and the professional. Emma made the case for having some friendships with colleagues:

> I have some very good friends who I see outside work and I think that we can still behave as colleagues in our place of work professionally and just switch in terms of our roles. Given that work makes up our life I think that it's important that you do have some people you consider friends. It is important to establish some sort of friendships. You could have quite a lonely existence otherwise because academia by its very nature can be quite lonely otherwise.

It is worth asking oneself the question 'Who would I turn to if I faced a major crisis or had to make a major decision in my working life?' Because our lives are so busy we tend to lose contact with friends we have been close to earlier in our careers. This in part explains the appeal of the website Friends Reunited. It is probably worth investing some time and effort to retain contacts with contemporaries whose careers have taken them elsewhere, for example, fellow doctoral students. They can give you the sort of dispassionate and detached advice that it might be more difficult for a colleague in your own department or university to provide.

Much of what has been discussed here relates to your own individual response to challenging events. However, it is important that universities and departments can provide a context within which fruitful interpersonal relationships can develop and flourish. Luke summarized the effective combination of personal initiative and supportive context well, arguing that collegiality was not an optional extra but was positively related to success:

> I think it helps to develop good personal relationships with colleagues. Again it depends from case to case. In some cases I've very good working relationships with people without knowing the first thing about them whereas others I'm quite close friends with. I don't suppose it's crucial. I think that collegiality is important. I think that departments that work well tend to be collegial and to be collegial there needs to be some interaction other than the professional. I don't think you all need to go bowling a couple of times a term or be forced to wear silly hats. But I think that it's part and parcel of professionalism that you cultivate the best relationship you can with somebody.

▶ Mentoring and appraisal

American books on academic career development devote whole chapters to the subject of mentoring, reflecting the fact that it is a more common practice in the United States. A distinction has to be drawn between formal mentoring systems, where a new entrant is linked with a more experienced member of staff who is expected to provide him or her with informal support and advice, and a situation where a new staff member chooses on his or her own initiative to develop an informal relationship with a more senior staff member. These arrangements are distinguished from those between a doctoral supervisor and a student, although the doctoral supervisor may continue to fulfil an informal mentoring role after the PhD has been obtained.

There is some American research that suggests that considerable benefits can be derived from mentoring. Lucas and Murry (2002, p. 24) report:

> Some research appears to confirm the notion that a mentorship in a faculty novice's first year is 'critical' in launching the person's productive career. Another analysis of recent vintage indicates that having a faculty mentor may very well remain important through-out at least the first three years of a newcomer's first appointment.

The downside of formal mentoring arrangements is that they convey 'a negative message that new members of the academy cannot be expected to succeed on their own, that they are incapable of seizing the initiative in seeking out senior colleagues for advice and guidance as necessary' (Lucas and Murry, 2002, p. 26). The most satisfactory mentoring arrange-ments may be those that arise spontaneously without the involvement of a third party. 'Mentoring arrangements that are truly functional must evolve "naturally" or spontaneously out of mutual professional attrac-tion. Ultimately their success comes to depend ... on some shared perception of common academic interests' (Lucas and Murry, 2002, p. 25). Rather than formally asking someone to be your mentor, a rela-tionship with a more senior colleague may develop in such a way that the functions of mentoring (support, practical advice, and so on) are fulfilled without the title being used.

Formal mentoring arrangements do not seem to have been very significant for many of our respondents, although they seem to work better in post-1992 universities, which may reflect more systematic support and a higher priority for them in those institutions.

In one case the experience was very negative, with the respondent perceiving that the mentor had become a bully. Lucy's experience was the most positive: 'I have had a mentor here and he's been very good. I haven't seen him much but he feels available and luckily the head of department this year and last year are both incredibly available and good at sorting things out.' The relative lack of importance of mentor-ing arrangements in many cases may not be accidental because the power relationships that exist within universities may not provide an environment that is conducive for them to succeed, unless the mentor and the new entrant can treat each other as intellectual equals. New entrants may be concerned that mentors will see them as a threat or

will exploit them through joint publications that do more to reinvigorate the mentor's career than kick start that of the new entrant. For
their part, mentors may be concerned about appearing patronizing or
out of touch to new entrants. As the university system and individual
disciplines undergo more rapid change, mentors may feel that their
skills and knowledge are irrelevant.

Much depends on whether collegiality or competitiveness prevails in
the relations within a department, emphasizing the need to find out as
much as you can about a department before you join it. Ruth placed an
emphasis on competitiveness 'and jealousy – a young academic with
ideas contributing to the field threatening colleagues who have been in
a department for a long time and are not producing very much'. In
contrast, one young lecturer discussing a department known for its
supportive environment commented:

> There is no secret at [X] apart from the fact that the department is hugely aware
> of the importance of protecting and fostering collegiality and certain profes-
> sional values. This means that all members of staff (including temporary lectur-
> ers) have an equal teaching and administrative load. Senior professors accept
> that part of their role is to mentor and support young members of staff, we have
> no free riders and generally we are friends as well as colleagues.

Unfortunately, many departments fall short of this standard and some
could be characterized as dysfunctional in terms of providing a
supportive environment for new staff. In such circumstances finding
your own mentor or mentors outside the department could be particularly valuable. Emotional support could be probably be provided more
effectively by one of your peers, but a more senior person may be able
to offer practical career advice and to provide opportunities for
advancement, as well as acting as a referee.

All universities have formal systems of appraisal. As Blaxter, Hughes
and Tight (1998, p. 202) note:

> Regular staff appraisal was imposed on the British higher educa-
> tion system by the former Conservative government as a condition
> for agreeing a pay award. Before that, few universities or colleges
> had formal appraisal systems in place: appraisal now forms an
> essential part of all institutions' quality assurance procedures.

Procedures that are imposed in this way can deteriorate into ritualistic
form filling exercises. Craig's comment was similar to that made by a

number of other respondents, 'They're really only lip service to ticking a box that needs to be ticked and forwarding a form that needs to be forwarded.' The view was also expressed that it could be both generalist and judgemental about effectiveness in a rather unhelpful way. However, appraisal arrangements can play a particularly important role in the successful completion of probation. The actual arrangements vary from one university to another but they usually involve a more senior member of staff who has undergone training to become an appraiser. The person being appraised fills in a standard form to which the appraiser adds comments. They then meet to discuss the form and agree concluding comments, including points for action in terms of additional training or support. Our respondents who had been appraised felt that they have derived some, but not a tremendous benefit from the appraisal process. Zoe could not remember what had happened at her appraisal a little over a year ago and thought that 'quite a few people tend to regard them as a sort of whingeing session'. Nevertheless, in Luke's case it helped him to make a crucial career decision:

> I don't know how useful it is to career development, it might be useful to some people. I find it quite a useful experience. The appraisal documentation is becoming fussier and fussier but there is something to be said for sitting down and writing these things out. It does help you to map out where you are and where you might be going. And it's not often that you have a dispassionate conversation with a senior member of the department about these broad career-type things so I found that quite useful. The first time I did it was at [a post-1992 university] where it was effectively suggested to me that maybe you can't get what you want at this institution. That was a remarkably honest thing for the university to say. It wasn't integral to my decision [to leave] but it certainly helped validate it.

New entrants do not have to rely entirely on the provisions made by formal university systems. It is probably a good idea to find time to appraise your own progress from time to time, to reflect about your personal and career development and the progress you are making in achieving your goals. Are there any areas in which progress is slower than you would like it to be? If so, why has this happened? Do you need to acquire new skills, and do you need to use your time more effectively? Is a particular line of research activity less promising than at one time seemed the case? Are you in the right institution or the right department? Difficult though it is, it is important to find time to stand back from the next immediate deadline and think systematically about whether you are moving in the right direction at the speed you would like.

It is also important to remember that there are sources of support available to you that are not linked to the institution. Lucy noted, 'we've got a very good union rep in the department and I find the presence of the union a positive aspect. Even though I haven't drawn on it for anything yet, I think it's a good force to have around.' Two formerly distinct unions covering higher education, the Association of University Teachers (AUT) and the National Association of Teachers in Further and Higher Education (NATFHE) are to merge from July 2006 as the Universities and Colleges Union with some 68,000 members in higher education. The work of the union is particularly relevant to problems of bullying and harassment, which unfortunately are far from being unknown in universities.

▶ Bullying and harassment

A significant number of our female respondents reported problems of bullying, harassment or inappropriate and unwelcome approaches from male colleagues. Ann commented:

> Being a young female with a bunch of men who are going through mid-life crises produces one sort of problem of its own; frequently I've had male colleagues make inappropriate suggestions and passes. They know how to deal with men, but young women creates its own problems for them.

These problems are certainly not unknown in university life, even if they are more prevalent in other sectors such as financial services. Blaxter, Hughes and Tight (1998, p. 188) state 'Increasingly, it is ... likely that you may feel that your manager, or a colleague, is bullying you.' One survey found that the RAE was perceived as putting increased pressure on university managers, which could lead to aggressive behaviour that filtered down to departments. One in ten university staff who responded to the survey said that the RAE was directly related to bullying in the academic workplace (*Times Higher Education Supplement*, 21 October 2005). From an American perspective, Penny Gold, writing in Goldsmith, Komlos and Gold (2001, p. 251) comments:

> The troubled territory of sexual relations in the academy looks different from the perspective of someone who's gone through academic life in a female body ... Virtually all academic women I

know experienced some remarks or seductive behaviour from professors when they were students, and it can continue into one's teaching career as an element in the differentially powered relationships between senior male and junior female faculty.

Although they often have a gendered dimension, incidents of bullying may often arise from a misuse of power rather than any sexual motive, or perhaps simply from too strong a belief in the benefits of experience and seniority. As the Health and Safety Executive has noted in its guidelines on stress in the workplace, bullying is bad, but is simply the most extreme example of problems in interpersonal relationships.

Many problems can be resolved before they become too serious if prompt action is taken. Lucy recalled:

> Last year there was a slight tension with a senior colleague who I'm not sure was fully supportive of the fact that I had different ideas from the course I was teaching on. There was a certain aspect of bullying. The department were very supportive about it and talked to the senior member of staff who apologized and it was sorted out quickly. The head of department at the time was fantastic about it, very supportive.

Ruth's account of her experience was more negative:

> [For] a period of probably two, two and a half years I was harassed and bullied by a senior female colleague in my department ... A resolution was reached in which it was agreed that I didn't take out a formal case against this woman ... it was an uneasy resolution. The university did not want to get involved in my view – they chose to ignore the problem.

Ruth wished she had taken 'specific action earlier on this harassment case as it wasted two years and [had] negative effects on my mental well-being and health'. There is much to be said for prompt action that can deal with a problem before it becomes too serious, but that is not to say that it is easy to act. For all their talk of community and collegiality, universities are hierarchical institutions. Heads of departments have to listen to what the person complained about has to say as well as the complainant, and decide between different interpretations of the same events. Formal procedures can be slow and cumbersome and could be a serious drain on the confidence and well-being of the complainant. In these circumstances a supportive mentor in another institution can be invaluable, while unions can provide relevant help and advice. You may wish to refer to the Health and Safety Executive's guidelines on stress, which cover relationship problems (http://www.hse.gov.uk/stress/index.htm). If you are going to make a formal complaint, keep a careful dated record of all relevant events and copies of all documents. Hopefully, you will not encounter problems of this kind, but it is best to be alert to such an eventuality.

▶ Conclusions

The external criteria for success that universities impose on their staff can mean that they can face conflicting and often seemingly unmanageable demands on their time. As Ruth noted:

> Myself and other people actually try to do all four tasks – research, teaching, administration and the professional service. And there not being enough time to do all of these four things, which has issues for long working hours ... The other issue would be the RAE, and this whole drive to produce outputs, to churn out the work, which diminishes the pleasure in doing the work in the first place. I'm left feeling that I'm just producing work at a very rapid pace.

As Amy commented, 'I've often thought I would tell my children not to become academics, or at least if you are going to become an academic, don't be blind about it.'

Your own integrity and sense of well-being will be enhanced if you are able to stay true as far as possible to the intellectual and social values that attracted you to academic life in the first place. If you feel satisfaction about the value of what you are doing, you will also be better placed to achieve more instrumental career goals. For all the difficulties that are encountered in an academic career, our respondents do not regret choosing it. As Maria commented, 'I enjoy it, it's fulfilling, although it is challenging, very challenging.'

In subsequent chapters we shall be examining how you can succeed in your teaching and your research, the two key components of your academic career. As we emphasized at the beginning of this chapter, there is no one formula that can bring you success. Definitions of what constitutes success may vary considerably from one person to another in the light of their own values and priorities. However, as Lauren pointed out, you should aim for quality rather than quantity in your work. She commented, 'If you're doing good work you'll achieve profile. The fact that you have many other strings to your bow is not going to disguise bad work.'

4 Teaching Effectively

Every academic expects to be engaged in teaching activities at university level. Even the most highly paid professor will expect to teach, however minimal the obligation. The amount of teaching you will be required to do will vary over time, and will depend on your particular career path, and the institutional context in which you find yourself. University teaching has shifted dramatically in the last decade or so, with quality audits somewhat guiding the way we now think about teaching, and the way in which we measure what is meant by effective teaching. We now have to prove much more that we are offering teaching of a high quality. We are judged by our department and university, and by the external funding and governing bodies of higher education. This has brought with it new stresses and strains on the profession, for both new entrants and more senior academics. Yet it is probably a greater strain on new entrants, who are perhaps less sure of themselves as teachers.

This chapter highlights some of the key issues associated with teaching in higher education. The first section considers the main factors that affect the way in which we can and do teach at university level. The second section focuses on the standards by which we judge what it means to be effective in teaching, and is followed by a discussion of whether formal training is useful to new entrants. Finally, this chapter offers some perspectives on the best ways to enjoy your role as a lecturer. However, although the chapter highlights some of the common problems associated with university teaching, the intention is not to provide a detailed guide to teaching techniques – that would be a chapter or book in itself. Some suggestions for further reading, advice and support are given at the end of the chapter.

▶ The learning environment

The approach of any lecturer, and particularly new entrants, to teaching will primarily be governed by the institutional context. As discussed in Chapter 2, there are obvious and subtle differences in the orientation and focus of UK universities. For those that are seen as more research-led, you may find that your teaching load is not too high in terms of the number of contact hours, compared to the more teaching-oriented institutions. No matter which type of university you work in, you may find that you are asked to teach at both undergraduate and postgraduate level, or that your teaching is concentrated in, or entirely in, one of these levels. You may also be required to team-teach, in other words, contributing to a course or module with colleagues, with one being responsible for the administration of that module, and a number of lecturers leading certain sessions. A slightly different but less common approach to team-teaching is when two (or more) colleagues work together on the teaching of a module, and are physically present together in the classroom.

In the early stages of your career, and especially in your first position, what you teach will be dictated by the requirements of the department. You may have been appointed to teach specific courses or modules, and these may reflect your research interests or might be broader survey courses at early undergraduate level. There may be little scope for negotiating what you teach at the early stage of your career, and you should be clear in your mind when applying for jobs, and/or at the interview stage, whether you are able and want to teach a particular course. Committing yourself or being asked to teach a core undergraduate module on an area tangential to your own interests and skills might require a significant amount of additional work in the writing of lectures and planning of seminars in a topic area that you are not necessarily up to date on. Whilst you may have to cope with such a situation, it is important to be mindful of the extra work this will entail. Depending upon the curriculum taught by your department, there may well be scope, even before you start your new position, and certainly within the first few years of your career, to propose the introduction of new courses or modules. You may feel that there is a gaping hole in the existing subject provision that you could fill. It is always a good idea to try to teach something that is specific to your interests. It may not always be possible, but if the institutional structures allow, it is worth pursuing. It may seem obvious, but working with a group of students on a subject area that you are interested in has certain added rewards for both yourself and the students, as presumably you will be more engaged with the topic. Having said that, academics do find that there are benefits from teaching a course or module that is less specific to their interests in that they (as well as the students) are working on a 'new' topic and therefore may have more empathy with the students as they get to grips with specific issues.

Research-led teaching

At present, there is great emphasis on research-led teaching at university level. Research-led teaching is nothing new within the university sector. However, it actually has a dual meaning. Traditionally, academics use research-led teaching to refer to research-based or research-informed teaching, whereby academics teach their specialist research areas, and share some of the insights gained from their research with students. Often, this type of research-led teaching is concentrated at the postgraduate level, with some activities at second or third undergraduate level. The second meaning of research-led teaching is currently 'in vogue' within universities, and refers to academics actively encouraging undergraduate students to carry out research within the parameters of a particular module. The emphasis is on undergraduates, as it is assumed that postgraduate students will be engaged in some research activities during their programme of study.

This type of 'action research' used to be primarily focused on the undergraduate dissertation. However, not all university programmes require students to undertake a dissertation, and the space pressures in the curriculum, particularly in semester-type systems, do not always allow for a dissertation. At present, examples of this type of research-led teaching can range from students executing a small piece of research on a topic defined by the tutor within a module, to a stand-alone extra-curricular project, for which students receive funding. In the United States, this type of research-led teaching is generally known as inquiry-based learning or undergraduate research, and is much more common than in the UK and continental Europe. The advantages of research-led teaching are the focus of another book in this series (Brew, 2006), where detailed examples of different kinds of research-led teaching are provided.

With UK universities seeking to re-emphasize to potential students the pivotal role of research, for both academics and students, this form of research-led teaching is becoming more common. It taps into both the pressures upon universities to recruit students – and 'research' is seen as a positive attraction to potential students – and the emphasis on the development of graduate skills. It is felt that this type of research-led teaching not only enhances student learning, in terms of both research skills and independent study skills, it also makes the student better appreciate the value of these graduate, key skills. The trend in encouraging undergraduate research-led teaching also acknowledges that universities are under increasing pressure, especially from the postgraduate funding bodies such as the ESRC, to equip undergraduates hoping to go on to further study with improved research skills that go beyond basic research methods courses or modules.

▶ Contracts and the student body

According to a recent AUT survey, 20 per cent of all academics are on teaching-only contracts. There were 29,000 academics on teaching-only contracts in 2003–4, compared with 15,000 for 2002–3. Of these, two-thirds were on fixed-term contracts, 80 per cent were working part-time, with 25 per cent only employed during term time (*Times Higher Education Supplement*, 24 June 2005). This not only indicates the changing nature of employment practices in academia, but also suggests that the RAE pressures are forcing universities to offer teaching-only contracts, and new entrants to take these positions. It also undermines the link between teaching and research, and is opposed to the current emphasis on research-led teaching. Clearly then, what you teach will be governed by the nature of your contract, and the scope for teaching in your research area may be limited by your terms of employment, or the university's orientation.

Other factors that affect the way in which academics approach their teaching relate to the students themselves. Different types of students have different needs when it comes to teaching. Each university has its own approach to the recruitment of the student body. At undergraduate level, student admissions will be governed by the entrance qualifications needed to secure a place on a degree course. Some universities are more attractive to overseas students than others, or a university will openly recruit from overseas. Other institutions actively recruit mature students onto undergraduate degree programmes. Student entrance requirements at postgraduate level also vary between universities, but less so than at undergraduate level. Again, there may be a greater emphasis upon overseas recruitment for Masters' programmes.

Student backgrounds
Thus, the approach to your teaching will have to take into consideration the composition of the student body. You need to be aware of the academic background of your students. Students need to be pushed if they are to benefit from their university learning, but there is little point

in being over-ambitious in terms of the level at which you pitch your teaching if you then leave behind the students in your class. This can be demoralizing for the students, and have knock-on effects for their performance in assessment and examinations. Questions may then be asked of you if the entire group is deemed not to be 'performing'. This can also be demoralizing for the lecturer. Zoe feels that her enjoyment as a lecturer is affected by the type of students, and stated that she has to deal with 'poor-quality students', and 'you don't feel it's worth your time teaching some of them'. It is therefore important to ascertain the ability and potential of your students, and work within those parameters. You should not be minimalist in your approach, but may need to adopt an incremental approach, building up the students' critical thinking skills and attainment.

There is some anecdotal comment amongst lecturers these days about the linguistic competence of overseas students, and the difficulties this raises for the student and lecturer. Despite strict language proficiency entrance qualifications set by each university, this appears to be a continuing problem. Normally, departments or the central administration of a university have a variety of support mechanisms in place that students can call upon, and you should familiarize yourselves with the support available to your students, so that you can point students in the right direction. There are cultural differences that need to be taken into account. Some cultures are less inhibited than others when it comes to participating in seminar discussions. It may not be that a student is struggling with a topic just because he or she is quiet in class, and as a lecturer, you need to be mindful of this. This is a very sensitive issue, because one of the skills we are requiring from students, or hoping to equip them with, requires them to actively participate. Therefore, you need to find appropriate ways to deal with this, and again you may need to seek advice from the university's support services.

Mature students also have different needs. Often they arrive at university enthusiastic and willing to learn, but lack confidence in their own abilities. It is a frequent comment from established lecturers how great mature students are, but that they need to be actively encouraged, with a little 'hand-holding' in the early stages of their university studies. Craig spoke of the satisfaction he derived from working with a student from a non-traditional ethnic minority background who was initially struggling with his work despite putting in great effort but eventually achieved marks at upper second level and gained entry to a MA programme. You also need to be aware of, if not sympathetic to, the context that students

find themselves facing. Increasingly, students have to find paid employment to fund their academic studies, and sometimes find it difficult to
balance the two. While a student should prioritize study over work, sadly
this is not always the case, and as a lecturer you have a professional, if
not moral, duty to ensure that students do not fall behind with their
academic studies.

These structural factors affect what you teach, and who you teach,
and will naturally also affect how you teach. With all of these issues to
consider, it becomes quite a melting pot of factors to take into account.
The need to ascertain the abilities and potential of students, as well as
cope with specific problems or characteristics of the ways in which
students approach their learning, need to be married with your own
ideas and standards of what constitutes effective teaching and learning. As you gain more experience of teaching, this becomes easier, but
for new entrants it is often a case of trial and error. It is important in
the early stages of your teaching to seek advice from colleagues or
dedicated staff in the wider university community. New entrants are
now required to undertake a specific postgraduate training course in
teaching, in which many of the issues will be discussed and possible
strategies offered (see below for more about training in teaching).

▶ Professional relationships with students

One of the main difficulties for a new entrant in approaching teaching
is coping with the sense of vulnerability you feel by being relatively
close in age to the students (or perhaps younger in the case of mature
students), something which Lauren highlights:

> I think that a lot of new entrants have a tendency, especially if they are quite
> young, to try to distinguish themselves from students in a way that suggests
> arrogance. There's a perfectly laudable attempt to try to assert some authority
> but it's not something that's necessary and students don't respond well to it.
> Students know perfectly well that you're young and that it's your first job and
> no matter what you do you're not going to disguise that. You have to know
> what you're talking about and also demonstrate that you know what you're
> talking about. I think a lot of people consciously or unconsciously try to assert
> themselves in a way that is not necessarily helpful.

Striking the right balance in terms of your relationship with students is
tricky. You need to be able to command some authority and respect

without being arrogant and perhaps alienating your students. You need to consider how you present yourself, the tone of your language, perhaps even what you wear. You should not try to pretend to be something that you are not, as this will be obvious. However, Lucy's advice to new entrants is 'not to be too friendly with students because I can see problems here where it's very difficult to tell some of the young staff apart from the students and I am not sure that those relationships are really appropriate'. It may be more difficult for female academics to find this balance, given that women are more prone to having judgements made on them because of their appearance. Being too friendly can cause problems, and it is certainly not advisable to go for a drink with the students that you teach in the early stages of your career. The way in which you work with students will evolve over time in a way that you are comfortable with, and that works for both yourself and the students. Again, if you are experiencing difficulties that you believe are due to your relative 'youth', it may be worthwhile seeking advice from others.

▶ Coping with your teaching load

In terms of the practical management of your teaching activities, one of the greatest difficulties for a new entrant is coping with your teaching load. Whilst your contact hours with students will be clearly timetabled, you also have to take into account the preparation and planning of teaching activities, dealing with students during your office hours, and increasingly responding to students via email. You will also have to decide how much of your teaching will be supported by an information technology (IT) platform. In terms of the preparation and planning of lectures and seminars, this can take a considerable amount of time in the early stages of an academic career. You may be writing brand new lectures, and should be reflecting and reviewing your techniques, particularly in seminars, and adjusting your approach accordingly.

As discussed in Chapter 3, there is an inherent danger in overpreparing. If you have a brand new lecture to write, this could consume your entire day. Most of those interviewed for this book have learnt by bitter experience. The trick is to set yourself a time limit, say three to four hours, for writing a lecture, and stick to it. By doing so, not only do you 'temper ambition' but you do not allow teaching preparation to encroach upon your other activities and commitments. Some academics write all their lectures and plan seminars well in advance of the new academic year, so that they can simply pull out their notes on the day. Others prefer to confine teaching preparation to a dedicated day a week. Others prefer to prepare the night in advance of the class so that it is fresh in their minds. It is obviously a matter of personal preference, finding out what works best for you. The preparation for teaching becomes easier over time, as you have built up a bank of resources, lecture frameworks, and seminar tasks that can be revised and adapted. However, the first few years can be tough, especially if you end up teaching different courses or modules each year. Added to this is the time you need to dedicate to marking essays and examinations, writing feedback on essays, and being available to discuss an essay with a student. Increasingly, students expect extensive feedback, and you will have to factor this into your work schedule.

Your accessibility to students also needs to be carefully managed. There is an expectation by some students that you should always be available for them. This is not always possible, and you should establish a defined policy on your own accessibility. You may wish to have specific office hours, or an open door policy. You might choose to actively encourage communication via email, or you may decide it is better to meet students face to face, and dissuade them from using email when wishing to discuss a specific issue with you. Again, this is a matter of personal preference, but you need to ensure you have a policy in place otherwise you could end up swamped with student enquiries at all times of the day (and night).

Using IT
The final issue to be examined in this discussion of the learning environment concerns the use of IT as a teaching tool, in other words beyond simple email communication with students. There are a variety of specialist educational platforms which enable you to set up discussion boards, blogs, have interactive lectures posted on a site, and allow students to carry out formative and summative assessment online. All of these can be extremely worthwhile as learning support tools. The reason for raising IT in this chapter is to simply note a word of caution. Firstly, you need to establish the capacity of IT provision at your university to furnish you with the tools you require. Secondly, unless you are favourably inclined to use these resources to support your teaching, you could end up doubling your workload. You need to decide whether to use such resources at all, and if so, to what extent you will use them, and whether you will require your students to use them. Otherwise,

you will end up duplicating your teaching and student support in the real and virtual environments.

Class organization: lecturing

How you actually teach a class is personal. You have to trial different ways of organizing a lecture or seminar, and decide what works for you and the students. As discussed above, how you approach your teaching will depend on the type of students you are working with, and the specific problems that you come across in class. However, there are common problems associated with teaching that most academics recognize and experience, particularly in the early states of their career. Ruth feels that:

> there is a constant tension between the student demand to be entertained in a class, and certainly my own desire that they should actually engage in a subject. I have asked students what they expect from a lecture for example – at least half of them said that they wanted to be entertained. So I guess it is finding a balance between getting the material across and keeping their attention.

Some academics adopt a deliberate strategy of 'entertaining'. Whilst this can be very appealing to students in terms of their enjoyment of a class, it is not advisable if you are not a good storyteller. Of course, we all enjoy a light-hearted anecdote, but it needs to be delivered well. In addition, some students grow tired of this approach, and start to question whether they have actually learnt anything in that particular session.

One of the biggest hurdles in lecturing is finding the right balance between having too much material for a lecture, and insufficient material. If you know a topic extremely well, it is often difficult to establish how much information and analysis the students require. Gauging what information the students need is easy to misjudge, and there is a fine line between simplifying the material and oversimplification of the lecture's content. It is important not to be over-ambitious in terms of the amount of material to be covered in a session. As Ruth stated: 'I always over-prepare and the students have said that I try to cover too much material in a particular module or even an individual lecture.' There is a natural tendency to over-prepare in the early stages of your teaching career. You will probably be writing lectures from scratch, and there is always a danger of trying to cover too many aspects of the topic. Therefore, it is a good idea to ask yourself, 'What are the key points I should discuss on this topic?' then compile your notes on these points only.

Another challenge of lecturing is finding mechanisms to get the students to think in the lecture, and not merely be passive learners – copiously taking down notes but failing to engage with what you are discussing. A useful means of getting the students to consider the arguments you put forward in a lecture is to clearly identify to them as the lecture progresses the difference between the factual knowledge you are providing and the analytical and interpretative perspectives. If you highlight this distinction, students will become accustomed to the nuances of your presentation, and hopefully will engage more critically with the material. Even though you might think a lecture has a standard format, you may find that breaking the lecture up with some short discussion with the students on a specific issue not only helps them to become more active learners, but also aids their concentration. Student involvement in lectures is dependent on the size and layout of the room, and the acoustics, as there is little point in asking for student comments if no one can hear them, yet it can be a useful technique.

Maintaining the students' attention span can be problematic, and by varying your approach within each lecture, you avoid being predictable, and hopefully keep the students' attention. It can be extremely off-putting for the lecturer to see a group of students begin a whispered conversation, or to see students passing notes around or sending text messages. While you may choose to ignore such conduct, some academics feel it is more effective to stop lecturing and ask the group to share their discussion (which might embarrass them and deter them in the future), or simply comment to the whole class that you are not prepared to continue until you have everyone's attention. You should avoid being too heavy-handed (after all these are young adults), but you may find it necessary to comment that their conduct is inappropriate.

Most educational research argues that a visual dimension in any learning environment assists the students in learning, and most academics recognize this. Visual aids – PowerPoint presentations, overheads, handouts, use of the whiteboard/blackboard, use of the Internet to highlight a point – can all play a valuable role in enhancing a lecture, and also help the student maintain concentration. However, again there is a fine line between a visual enhancing a point you are making in a lecture and distracting from it, but you will soon establish the boundary as it will be clear from the reaction of students whether the point is clear. It is important not to overload the students with information on a slide or overhead – confine yourself to succinct points and pointers, which you elaborate on verbally. If not, the student will be focused on writing everything down, will not be listening, and there-fore will not be engaging with the topic, although it can be helpful to post slides or overheads on the module web page before the lecture.

One of the most obvious points of lecturing is being heard, and you must establish whether you are audible. So often, lecturers do not think to check that they can be heard, and students tend to be reluc-tant to ask a lecturer to speak up. Not only do you need to learn to throw your own voice, without shouting, but you also need to take into account the acoustics of each room that you teach in.

Class organization: seminars

Seminar teaching brings with it different challenges, the main one being how to encourage students to participate. This can be extremely testing, particularly for a new entrant. There will always be some students in a seminar group more reluctant to contribute to plenary discussions than others, and there are usually one or two students in a group who tend to dominate the seminar. You have to find ways of encouraging everyone to participate, as this is central to their learning experience. There is often a tendency for the quieter students to rely on their more vocal peers in the group, and if you have a particularly quiet seminar group, you may very well come to rely on the more willing discussants – just to break the silence.

There are some straightforward techniques that can be used in the seminar room. A useful approach for establishing a conducive learning environment is to get students to appreciate that they are in a group, will be in that group for the semester or year, and should consider themselves a team, and thus establish a group-working ethic. This creates a more positive environment, and also encourages students to be accountable to each other as well as the lecturer. In addition to this, it is a good idea is to establish expectations with the group at the start of the academic year. You can ask students what they expect from the seminars, and then outline what you expect, and draw up a sort of learning contract. Some literature on teaching techniques actually recommends that you draw up a paper learning contract based on this discussion, signed by yourself and the students. It is argued that if non-participation or poor attendance becomes a persistent problem, you could pull out the contract and remind the student of his or her obli-gations. This may seem a little extreme to some, but the basic princi-ple is a valuable one. By making it clear to students from the outset that you expect them to prepare for, attend and participate in each and every seminar, you can circumvent the pitfalls in seminar teaching.

To make seminars more beneficial to student learning, you should consider varying the types of activities in each seminar. Whilst plenary discussion has an important role to play, and develops students' communication skills, diluting this with small group work can be extremely worthwhile for the students (and yourself). Group work can take a variety of forms – you can set groups the same task or different tasks, you can pair off students then merge pairs into larger groups, or you could have only two groups (see further reading for a wide variety of tips on seminar teaching). However you chose to organize the group work though, there are two important points. Firstly, you need to provide instructions to the students on the activity. However, in some cases you might not want to be too prescriptive as part of the task is for students to make critical judgments about how to approach the task. Secondly, you need to effectively manage the reporting back process. All students will want an opportunity to present their findings and so on, but this can become repetitive if you have four or five groups reporting back, and often the other students lose concentration. To avoid this, you could ask students to summarize the group's findings on an overhead, and simply present the salient points, and hopefully avoid repetition. Alternatively, you could travel around the class, asking each group to report to you, and take on the role of verbally summarizing the findings of that particular task.

The final common problem in seminar teaching, although it can occur in the lecture hall too, is how to ask the question. Open-ended questions are seen as more useful to stimulate discussion. Closed questions by their very nature shut down the opportunity for debate. However, it may be that the question is too 'open', and that students misinterpret or misunderstand what you are asking them, or possibly don't understand at all. You have to ensure, probably through trial and error, that the question you ask is pitched correctly.

There are a wide variety of techniques that you can use in your teaching (see further reading), and you may be exposed to these through postgraduate training in teaching. Not only should you trial different ways of teaching, and find the ones that work for you, but you should also try to vary the techniques both within a session and between sessions. Some academics argue that they stick to one method because it works for them, and this is perfectly understandable. However, there is also evidence to suggest that students benefit much more from their learning if they are exposed to a variety of techniques. It is always a good idea to plan in detail each seminar session, and by doing so you have a written account of the techniques that worked in the past, and thus a resource that you can draw upon in future planning. Good seminar planning can also circumvent the problem of non-participation by students as you can get all students involved in small group activities, if not plenary discussions. However, you do need to approach your planning with a degree of flexibility so that you can deal effectively with the unplanned. You may find that, for example, one week your seminar group is reluctant to participate, so you plan for the following week using alternative techniques to encourage student contributions. Yet at the next class, within the first few minutes, it is clear that students have much to say on the topic, and you will therefore need to adjust your plan so as not to deter them from participating.

It is so important to evaluate your own teaching. As discussed in this chapter, how your teaching evolves over time is a matter of trial and error. Sitting down and thinking about what your aim was for a particular session, why you chose the approach you did, and then reflecting upon the reasons why something worked, and why something else was not so positive, is an important element of being an effective teacher.

▶ Standards in teaching

You would have to be tremendously thick-skinned not to come out of a seminar that did not go very well and not consider the reasons that students were unwilling to discuss the issues, or respond to your questions. Even if you have the skin of an elephant, it may be that there is a persistent problem in your teaching approach, which you will not be able to ignore. Judgements about how effective you are as a lecturer are multi-level. In the current framework of internal and external audits on the quality of teaching, we have to both demonstrate and be sure that we are being as effective as possible in our teaching. Arguably, the best judge of your standard of teaching is yourself. You know what you did in a particular session, you have some idea of the student's capacities and abilities, and you are aware of the bigger picture – in other words, how a particular session fits into the module or course overall. By reflecting upon your own practice, you are able to make considered judgements about the standards of your own teaching, and perhaps adjust your own practices if needs be.

However, you are not the only one judging your performance as a lecturer. Students can be the harshest critics of your effectiveness as a lecturer. Students expect a certain standard of teaching, and seem quite happy to complain if they do not feel you are up to scratch. They rarely tell you in person, but instead seek out your head of department. In most universities, students are asked to complete end-of-year evaluations of their modules. Again, if they feel that the lecturer was not performing by their standards of effectiveness, they tend to be more than willing to give unfavourable evaluations. These evaluations are reviewed, generally by the head of department, or by a teaching quality committee within the department. It is usually at this point that you can defend your own teaching – there may have been particular problems with a set of students. However, students may not be judging their lecturer on his or her ability to teach, but on entertainment value, or on the fact that they received poor marks for essays, or more importantly, their misunderstanding of the aims and objectives of the module. It is often quite hard to establish whether there is an inherent problem with a lecturer's approach to teaching, or whether it is simply a clash of personalities. As stated above, only you really know the truth, and you may find it quite difficult to deal with what you see as unfair criticism.

It is now common for university departments to set up their own mentoring schemes. Sometimes these include support for teaching. Alternatively, departments establish a 'buddy'-type system for teaching, whereby colleagues are paired and asked to observe each other's teaching. For a new entrant, this can seem quite daunting – to have a new colleague come and observe you in the classroom. However, if organized in the right way, that is, making sure that colleagues at roughly the same stages of their career are paired together, these observations can be a useful mechanism for obtaining feedback on your teaching. Our respondents were generally positive about the practice of teaching observation, seeing it as a useful way of exchanging ideas and learning from others. Teaching observations are also an important part of postgraduate training in teaching: see below.

It is a quirk of all of us – we are quite happy to teach to a group of students, we are comfortable delivering conference papers in front of our peers, but having a colleague observe our teaching makes us feel nervous and uncomfortable. This is probably because teaching observations create a false environment – there is an additional person in the room – and both you and the students are aware of this. The first time you are observed is the worst, but subsequent observations seem less nerve-racking. Obtaining constructive feedback on your teaching approach from a colleague is extremely valuable, and observations are a useful means of assuring yourself that your teaching is effective.

External audit of teaching

Every university has a governance structure to ensure that academic standards of teaching are adhered to. Some universities review individual departments on a rolling basis, requiring them to submit documentation to prove the quality of their teaching. With the reforms to higher education came the Quality Assurance Agency's (QAA) new approach to reviewing the quality of higher education teaching. This took the form of subject reviews, in which every university department was audited. It became quite a paper-generating exercise, with departments having to supply a self-assessment document on their teaching provision, supported by boxes of materials to support their claims. The QAA process required departments to demonstrate quality not only in terms of teaching and assessment of students, but in the merits of the curriculum, the support given to students, and the learning resources available to students. This culminated in a week-long inspection by a group of colleagues in the discipline from other universities, observing teaching, talking to students, and rating the quality of provision under headings.

To the relief of many, the QAA recognized the resource-intense nature of the subject reviews, and has since moved to a 'lighter touch' approach, whereby the institution is inspected, and certain departments are identified as having to provide some evidence of teaching quality. While the system may well be revised again, external auditing will remain. In this context, it is advisable to keep electronic and paper records of anything pertaining to your teaching and support for student learning. Even without rigorous external auditing, there will be a point at which an internal university review will be carried out into the teaching quality provision on your department. In addition, you will probably have to supply evidence of teaching quality in promotion applications at a later stage of your career.

▶ Being 'trained' as a lecturer

Until the early 1990s, there were relatively few opportunities or requirements for formal training in higher education teaching. New entrants into the profession simply had to rely on memories of their own time at university, and recall for themselves what worked and what didn't work in the seminar room or lecture hall. They may have had some experience of seminar teaching whilst completing their doctorate, and may have received some guidance from their supervisor on teaching strategies, but this was *ad hoc* and very much dependent upon the department's own approach to postgraduate training. Once they were appointed as lecturers, there might have been the possibility to attend staff development events within the university, but that was all.

Higher education teaching was 'revolutionized' in the 1990s with the introduction of postgraduate-style teaching qualifications. This was primarily in response to increased government pressure for universities to demonstrate teaching quality. Postgraduate training courses began as a voluntary means by which new entrants could engage in some formal teaching training, but swiftly became compulsory for new entrants in most universities. The Higher Education Academy, successor body to the Institute of Learning and Teaching, seeks to establish professional standards in teaching and learning, not least with guidelines for postgraduate training courses. Young academics may wish to consider whether it is worthwhile being recognized by such bodies (www.heacademy.ac.uk). The introduction of postgraduate teaching certificates for new entrants, although not necessarily restricted to new entrants, was primarily a reflection of external audit pressures, but also tapped into the notion that just because you can research, it does not mean that you can teach. Being able to communicate your ideas and research in writing, or by presenting conference papers to your peers, does not necessarily make you an effective communicator with a student audience. It was recognized that some training ought to be given, particularly to new entrants, aiming to circumvent the status quo. As Luke comments:

> I think that one of the reasons that these teaching certificates are so common-place is to disabuse people of the notion that there's an automatic received wisdom that's passed down the generations; this is the way you do it.

Postgraduate teaching courses for lecturers are generally organized and run by the staff development and/or education departments within each university, and often last for a year, with a mixture of group sessions and independent study. Normally, these courses involve both theoretical and practical elements. Participants are generally required to familiarize themselves with some of the academic literature on higher education which deals with both theories of learning, and approaches and styles of teaching, as well as participating in teaching observations, designed so that young lecturers obtain some feedback on their teaching style and approach and perhaps observe others. The balance between these two elements depends on the university's approach to training, but both theory and practice are included.

Most of those interviewed for this book had undertaken a post-graduate teaching course, and the majority felt that one of the benefits of these teaching courses was meeting their peers from across their university, which they probably would not have done otherwise, given that academics tend to function primarily within their own department and have few dealings with colleagues outside their cognate disciplines. The other benefit of these courses is being exposed to new techniques on how to teach, and sharing ideas with peers on common problems in the lecture hall or seminar room. Often this builds up your own confidence as you realize that the difficulties you are experiencing with a student group are not necessarily particular to you. Luke felt that the value of the teaching certificate was in discussing the fact that students learn differently and 'that students have very different agendas from those we present them with and in many ways the task of being successful is to find ways of reconciling their agenda with your agenda'. Ruth wryly commented that the postgraduate training course she undertook:

> benefited my teaching by realizing what it was to be on the other side of the classroom, and to re-experience what it is to be on the end of really bad teaching. It gave me a certain empathy towards my students and spurred me on to make my modules more interesting, and specific classes more interesting and varied, and to test out new things and be more innovative.

While Ruth may have been unfortunate not to find the teaching of her course very inspiring, the point about remembering what it is like to be a student is an important one.

However, there appears to be a growing resentment amongst academics required to undertake a postgraduate training course in teaching. All those interviewed for this book had mixed views about the value of these courses. Craig thought that the teaching certificate he had taken was 'not really very useful at all. When it's provided by the institution, paradoxically it tends to be very badly taught, people switch off and feel coerced into doing it.' Maria thought that the certificate she took was too 'one size fits all' in character and took insufficient account of the particular requirements of her discipline, English, which involved a lot of work based on the examination of texts. The *Times Higher* recently reported the growing dissatisfaction amongst lecturers at the start of their careers about teacher training, stating that they were dismissing their training as a waste of time (*Times Higher Education Supplement*, 22 April 2005). This disquiet centres around three issues. The first is time. The demands on the time of an academic, and especially a new entrant, are ever increasing. RAE pressures, teaching loads and administrative duties vary across universities, but most academics feel that the expectations of them are rising. Being asked to undertake a postgraduate teaching course for a year (or more) only adds to this pressure of time management. Second, and probably as a result of the additional time burden of training, is the general feeling that a specific and lengthy course is unnecessary. Most new entrants will have some experience of teaching, and therefore do not feel there is much point in their undergoing further intensive training. However, the third and seemingly dominant reason for the growing resentment at having to be trained as a lecturer is the nature of these postgraduate courses. As stated above, most of these courses require participants to immerse themselves in the theoretical literature on teaching in higher education. It is not always clear at the time of undertaking such a course why this is necessary, and it is perceived as a waste of time. New entrants' expectations of these courses are that they will be given guidance and tips on teaching, and they do not necessarily expect (or want) to write essays on the conceptual issues associated with student learning.

In addition, as Maria observed, postgraduate teaching courses tend to be generic, in the sense that they are not tailored to your discipline. Approaches to teaching naturally vary across disciplines, and therefore a young history lecturer, for example, does not necessarily see any value in discussing teaching techniques used in chemistry. Lucy reflects this general tension about postgraduate teaching certificates:

> This is my tenth year of teaching and I'm not particularly sure that sitting in a room with scientists and talking about lab work helps me understand my teaching. I'm very willing to go on courses about teaching, I want to learn new approaches, how to deal with problems, I would be delighted to do that, but I do think they need to be slightly more specific towards what the department wants and your discipline.

This is a key problem, which is beginning to be recognized by universities. There are moves in some institutions to revise postgraduate teaching certificates so that they are more discipline-specific, either by structurally organizing the delivery of these courses into groups (social science and humanities together, natural sciences together), or by moving some of the training provision into departments themselves. This is obviously resource-dependent, and any revisions to the existing approach to the training of academics in teaching will depend on the individual university.

However, with the growing unrest among lecturers, there is a possibility that the governing bodies of university higher education may force the hand of institutions in the near future and require them to revise their postgraduate courses to be more discipline-oriented. It may well be that academics would be more predisposed to undertaking such training if it was perceived to be more tailored to their needs, and would therefore not resent quite so much the additional demands upon their time. Philippa Sherrington undertook a postgraduate course in higher education teaching in the mid-1990s, and recognizes all of the criticisms made about the nature of these courses. However, in hindsight, she feels that there is some value in generic courses, in that they enable you to recognize what is appropriate for you in terms of teaching methods and approaches. For example, by being involved in a lengthy discussion on the use of structured questions utilized in the natural sciences, she was able to evaluate these and decide their appropriateness for her discipline. Generic courses help you to establish what is fitting. Moreover, although having to read and synthesize a good deal of academic literature on the conceptual frameworks of student learning was demanding at the time, it has proved to be extremely valuable as Philippa's career progressed, enabling her to better appreciate some of the fundamental issues in learning, and deal with specific learning and teaching problems in arguably a more effective way.

▶ Conclusions

Establishing yourself as an effective lecturer in higher education is not straightforward, but as with most things in life, we learn by experience, and it becomes easier. However, difficulties can arise at any point during your career – having to teach a course or module that does not really interest you, having to cope with a 'difficult' student, or struggling to balance your teaching commitments with a current research project. The higher education environment means that we are continually called to account for our teaching. In some ways, this is positive, as it forces us to reflect upon our own practices. In other ways, it adds to the pressures on our time and can cause some resentment, perhaps making us less effective as teachers. As discussed above, preparation and planning are key to becoming effective in your teaching, and self-reflection helps us to learn from our experiences in the lecture hall or seminar room.

From those interviewed for this book, and from talking to colleagues and friends in the profession, it seems that the most important factor in effective teaching is enjoyment. Working with a group of students can be both rewarding and pleasurable. You are not only guiding them through their learning, but actually seeing the results of their learning over a period of time, not just in their final essay and examination results, but in the ways they develop in the classroom. They may become more confident in participating in seminar discussion, you may see that they have improved their written skills as a result of your feedback, and hopefully you will see them mature in terms of their level of critical thinking. As Mike commented, 'The goal of this level of education is to produce people that are independent thinkers, critically analysing material.' You can also learn from students – listening to their ideas and thoughts may challenge your own thinking on a topic, or may inspire you to explore an issue further in your own research. As discussed, while you may find that you are more effective when teaching in your own area of expertise or research, the rewards from working with a group of students are not confined to research-led teaching.

Establishing a good rapport with your students is certainly necessary to both their and your enjoyment of learning and teaching, but you need to conduct yourself in a professional manner. You want to be approachable, to be seen as a mentor rather than a 'teacher', but also need to establish with the students what is expected from them. By defining these expectations, you should be able to have a productive relationship with the students that you work with, facilitating their learning, and gaining professional satisfaction as you see them develop.

▶ Further reading and sources of advice

Some useful sources on teaching approaches are Brown and Race (2002), Edwards, Smith and Webb (2001), Entwistle (1988), Gibbs and Habeshaw (1989), Jarvis, Holford and Griffin (2003), Jenkins, Breen and Lindsay (2003), Maier and Warren (2000), Race (2001) and Squires (2003).

Helpful discipline-based advice and support can be obtained from the Higher Education Academy's Subject Network, which is made up of 24 subject centres (http://www.heacademy.ac.uk/SubjectNetwork.htm). These aim to improve the student learning experience in higher education through the development and transfer of good teaching and learning practices. The work of the English Subject Centre received particular praise from our respondents in post-1992 universities.

5 Supervising and Examining PhD Students

You should not be involved in supervising or examining PhD students when you are in an entry-level post as a postdoctoral fellow, contract researcher or temporary lecturer because you would not be able to see the PhD through to completion. Even when you have obtained a permanent post, the extent to which you are involved in PhD supervision will depend to a large extent on the nature of the university and department you find yourself employed in. A large research-oriented department may have a considerable number of PhD students, and the department culture and the need for supervisors is likely to involve you in supervision at a relatively early stage of your career. In a post-1992 university with a stronger teaching emphasis there may be very few PhD students and you may not be required to undertake any supervision. Indeed, the extent to which you are interested in PhD supervision may influence the type of post you apply for. Even if you do not expect to be involved in PhD supervision in the immediate future, you need to be aware of the challenges and opportunities that PhD supervision presents. As Delamont, Atkinson and Parry comment (1997, p. 1):

> Supervising doctoral students is one of the most satisfying things that anyone in higher education can do. Watching a new scholar become an independent researcher, conduct a project, write up the results, present them at a conference and see their first publications is a wonderful experience.

Different ways of structuring supervision
PhD supervision may be structured in a number of different ways in a department (the different models may coexist within a department):

- The sole supervisor who supervises a student within his or her specific area of expertise. The sole supervisor is usually a relatively senior scholar with an established reputation in a particular field. The PhD student is seen as undergoing an apprenticeship with the supervisor. Indeed, the student may subsequently obtain employment as a research assistant with the supervisor. This is very much the 'traditional' model of supervision, but has not been completely displaced.

- Increasingly departments appoint a second supervisor to work alongside, but in a subordinate position to the senior supervisor, or even have a team of supervisors. One reason for doing this is to have someone who knows the student's work if the supervisor falls ill, takes an appointment elsewhere or goes away on study leave. However, it can also provide a form of training for more junior staff. How well this works depends on how interested the senior person is in providing some systematic form of training and how involved the junior supervisor is in the supervision process. In other words its success as a form of socialization can be very 'hit and miss'. However, it is less daunting than suddenly being made the sole supervisor for a student. If it is not a practice that your department follows, it may be worth suggesting it.

- Another form of supervision is where there are two joint supervisors who have an approximately equal role in supervision. This may be particularly suitable when the two supervisors can bring complementary skills to the supervision of the thesis. For example, one supervisor may be expert in a particular country or region of the world and the other supervisor may have a 'functional' expertise that cuts across a number of countries. Or perhaps one supervisor may have a methodological expertise that is relevant to the thesis while the other supervisor may be knowledgeable in the substantive area being covered by the thesis. Undertaking this form of supervision may be a useful bridge between being the junior supervisor and taking the responsibility of lead or sole supervision. However, you need to be sure that you can have a satisfactory working relationship with the other supervisor. You should discuss your respective roles and how the supervision process will operate before embarking on it.

- UK universities have not generally moved to the American model, also used extensively elsewhere in Europe, of a dissertation committee. The Quality Assurance Agency's (QAA) code of practice on postgraduate research programmes envisages that each student will have one main supervisor but 'He or she will normally be part of a supervisory team' (QAA, 2004, p. 14). However, the code of practice does not specify how this supervisory team might be composed or how it might operate.

▶ The advantages and disadvantages of supervision

There are a number of reasons that you may want to take on PhD supervision or examining (examining is discussed more fully later in the chapter). It may present an opportunity to develop your own research work through engaging in a sustained dialogue with someone who is undertaking work related to it. For example, it may enable you to explore an aspect of your work or a related topic that you do not have time to investigate yourself. You may see being appointed as a PhD supervisor as a 'rite of passage', as a recognition that you have finally arrived as an academic. Your department may provide you with incentives to undertake PhD supervision, for example, a reduction in other forms of teaching.

However, it is important to be cautious before you eagerly accept the role of PhD supervisor. PhD supervision is a highly specialized form of teaching that requires particular skills which are different from other forms of providing learning. You could be a very good lecturer and seminar tutor, but much less effective at PhD supervision. If you are unsuccessful, the consequences are more visible and more serious than if one student fails a module that you have taught. Lauren warned:

> Be very choosy about the PhD students you accept and those you accept to examine. I think that when you are new on the block and someone asks you to supervise a PhD student or particularly to examine one you are actually rather flattered, it's a sign that you've arrived. The instant reaction is to say yes and I think that can be really dangerous.

Similarly, Luke warned against viewing all prospective PhD students as if they are a newly minted version of the prospective supervisor:

> The ability range among PhD students is probably wider than you first realize. You tend to think they're all as good as you were because by definition if you're an entry-level lecturer you were a reasonably good PhD student.

Here are some basic rules to observe when considering a PhD application you have been asked to supervise:

- Don't be pressurized to supervise outside your area.
- Try to ensure that if the applicant does not speak English as a first language, he or she is reasonably proficient in English as a medium of communication. There is nothing more frustrating than dealing with students who are intellectually able but unable to express themselves sufficiently well in the language of examination. Stipulating a particular standard in English language tests does not necessarily deal with this problem.
- If it is not possible to interview the applicant face-to-face at least try and talk to him or her by telephone or by email. This will help you to assess his or her proficiency in English and enable you to make an assessment of the student as a person, which is particularly important given the one-to-one nature of most supervision.
- As Luke put it, 'Don't just take somebody because they're working in your area, take somebody who works in your area and looks like they are very good.'

Supervision and time management

It is also important to bear in mind that PhD supervision can have important implications for effective time management. PhD supervision is a very 'lumpy' activity that can place variable but heavy demands on your time. This reflects the lifecycle of the PhD to a certain extent. While the student is defining the scope of the PhD and undertaking a literature review, a considerable amount of guidance is usually necessary. Students often want to undertake topics that are hopelessly ambitious if the thesis is going to be completed within four years, if ever. In the second year of research, students are likely to be undertaking field research or working in archives and this may well take them away from the home university. While it is important to keep an eye on their progress and discuss problems they have encountered, they are likely to need less intensive supervision during this period. When they have completed their data collection and start to write up, they will once again need more regular guidance. The problem with PhD theses is that they are rather like buses; they tend to come along in groups. There is nothing more daunting from a time management perspective than suddenly finding that one has three complete PhD drafts to read.

How can one avoid such a situation? First, it is important not to take on too many PhD students to supervise. The QAA states that

'Institutions will ensure that the quality of supervision is not put at risk as a result of an excessive volume and range of responsibilities assigned to individual supervisors' (QAA, 2004, p. 17). However, no specific guidance is provided on how 'excessive' responsibilities might be identified. Universities and departments usually have maximum norms in terms of the number of students that can be supervised, but these are often rather on the high side. They often seem to be influenced by the experience of the natural sciences where PhD students work as part of a research group in the laboratory, exploring different aspects of a shared problem in a way that produces economies of scale. If you have, say, eight PhD students, you may not be able to claim all the teaching relief to which you are entitled. You need therefore to set your own personal limit, taking account of all the relevant circumstances. Three or four PhD students is likely to be more than enough for most supervisors. If possible, you should try to stagger their starting dates: that is, do not take on four students in one year. This should even out the demands arising at different points of the PhD cycle, although one may encounter a phenomenon similar to buses whereby a bus that starts later catches up the bus in front that has picked up all the passengers. PhD students work at different paces, so students with different starting points may converge on a similar finishing point. This is another reason for not having too many PhD students.

You also need to think about the pattern of contact with the student. As suggested above, this will be partially affected by the lifecycle of the thesis. The QAA recognizes that 'The nature and frequency of contact between student and supervisor(s) will vary, depending on the duration of the programme, the way research is being conducted and the amount of support needed by the student' (QAA, 2004, p. 18). It also notes that 'Institutions may find it helpful to include in their code(s) of practice ... guidance on the minimum frequency of contact advisable between students and supervisors' (QAA, 2004, p. 17). Whatever is said in a code of practice, it is important to establish an agreed pattern of contact with each student from the start of the supervision. In the natural sciences, if you want to see the student, you simply go to his or her laboratory bench. In the humanities and social sciences, it is literally possible for the student to 'disappear'. You need to agree a regular pattern of meetings with the student, which may be varied over the lifecycle of the thesis.

One other general point to bear in mind is that there are many acceptable styles of PhD supervision, and you should settle for one that suits you. As has been suggested elsewhere in this book, the most comfortable and generally the most successful way to work is to be true to your own values and preferences. Good PhD students will recognize and accept that there are different styles of supervision. Robinson experienced a change of supervisor during his PhD because his first supervisor left the university:

> The key point which emerged from this change of supervision was that as a supervisor she ought not to be judged by the criteria I had used to judge her predecessor. Supervisor number one was gregarious and outspoken. Her successor was quiet and methodical. From the comments which I received, each was highly effective, but in different ways.
>
> (Robinson, 1997, p. 81)

▶ Managing PhD students

PhD students have to be managed if they are to successfully complete their PhD. They also have to be managed to ensure that they do not make excessive demands on your time. Having successfully supervised PhD students will certainly be taken into account in internal promotions to senior lecturer in a research university. However, it will not compensate for the absence of the four strong publications needed for the RAE.

It is important to recognize that this is a structured relationship between two people in the traditional model, a model that is likely to persist at least to some extent given the emphasis that the QAA places on the role of the 'main supervisor'.

Like any relationship between two people, it can succeed or fail and it can change over time. Dunleavy (2003, p. 7) warns that relations between a supervisor and a PhD student can often go wrong. The supervisor may become 'neurotic about a younger rival encroaching on her terrain' or the student may lose confidence in the supervisor's ability. 'Or they may become too close, with the supervisor being so dominant in the relationship that the student becomes a mere disciple.' One of the keys to successful supervision is achieving a successful balance in the relationship. The student must be guided, but not so much that his or her autonomy is sacrificed. The student must be supported, but not so much that a close friendship displaces a professional relationship.

The variability of PhD students

The relationship between supervisor and student is a professional relationship with a particular purpose: the successful achievement of a PhD. Although it is constrained by university rules and by informal norms and understandings, the relationship with each PhD student will be different. Each student comes to the relationship with his or her own personal and intellectual history, preconceptions and expectations. Indeed, supervising a PhD student is in large part an exercise in expectations management. If you have good people skills, this will help you to recognize where a particular PhD student is coming from and to pick up on significant cues in what may appear to be insignificant statements.

Luke offered good advice in this respect:

> PhD students are not a generic type, some of them are very self-motivated, very easy to get on with in the sense that they will know exactly what is expected of them, they will be very good at managing their time, they will be well equipped with the conceptual, theoretical and methodological resources that they need. In effect the trick is to find out about your student and his or her abilities and aptitudes very early. The way in which I work with PhD students varies considerably from student to student. It's really about knowing the particular needs of the student.

It is useful to think about how the student might see the relationship with the supervisor. The student might be disappointed to have been allocated to a relatively junior member of staff, but he or she might come to appreciate that such a person might have more time for him or her than a 'star' who is always travelling around the world to conferences. If you have followed the advice given earlier and only selected students whose work is relevant to yours, they will appreciate being able to talk to someone who is a real expert in the field in which they are working. However, the student will quickly become more knowledgeable than you on the particular topic on which he or she is working. Your task is not to match that detailed knowledge but to ensure that:

- There is an underlying core theme drawing the thesis together: 'the thesis must have a thesis'.
- Proper and sufficient use is made of primary evidence.
- Relevant theory is developed and deployed throughout the thesis.
- The thesis has a clear and coherent structure.

- Irrelevant and superfluous material is excised from the thesis. As Burnham notes (1997a, p. 8), 'The ability to highlight the essential and discard the peripheral is in many ways the key to a successful PhD.'
- Appropriate methodologies are used and their use and limitations are discussed in the PhD.
- The thesis is clearly expressed and is free of grammatical errors and spelling mistakes.
- The bibliography is thorough and properly presented.
- The student is aware of submission deadlines and practises effective time management.

Challenging students

Three types of student can pose particular difficulties for the supervisor. The bugbear of all supervisors is the student who is not responsive to advice. Of course, all PhD students are unresponsive to advice to some extent. A standard piece of PhD student folklore is 'Never do or believe exactly what your supervisor tells you' (Page, 1997, p. 55). To some extent, such scepticism is necessary. Part of becoming a successful academic is developing your own distinctive 'voice'. This will not happen if the PhD student does not secure a measure of autonomy from the supervisor. Nevertheless, this must not be taken too far. As Page admits (1997, p. 55): 'Sometimes listen to your supervisor, pure chance says they'll give sound advice from time to time.' It may be helpful to make a clear distinction between advice that is obligatory and advice that is permissive. In other words, there are times when you have to say to the student, 'If you don't follow my advice on this point, there is a real danger that your thesis will be referred.' On other points you may say, 'My advice is this, but it is your decision whether you follow it or not.' It is good practice to have an agenda at supervision meetings and an agreed note of their outcome sessions, with a list of points to be followed written up by the student as minutes and subsequently signed by both the supervisor and student.

The opposite of the student who will not accept or respond to advice is the PhD student who expects to complete a 'painting by numbers' thesis. In other words, the student wants to be told what the structure of the thesis should be, what should go into each chapter and which archives should be consulted or persons interviewed to yield the necessary data. Such a student has not really made a satisfactory transition from being an undergraduate to being a research postgraduate, despite the usual intervention of an MA with a dissertation requirement. There are some students who can succeed very well up to MA level, but encounter difficulties once they embark on a PhD. These problems are very difficult to spot during the recruitment and selection process because the student often has an excellent record of progress up to that stage.

This presents a real challenge in expectations management. If at all possible, you should try to find out what is the root of the problem. Does the student regard the supervisor as an oracle and want to become his or her disciple? In an age in which deconstruction is widely legitimized, this might seem unlikely, but it does happen. In some cases, it may be the result of a cultural background that encourages veneration for older, knowledgeable individuals. Particular personality types may like being dependent on an authority figure. This is not an easy situation to deal with it, but it needs to be pointed out to the student, as tactfully as possible, that a PhD is meant to be an exercise in original scholarship and one cannot be original if one does not develop sufficient independence of mind. One can be influenced by a particular individual's work while at the same time approaching it in a critical spirit.

Self-confidence and motivation

Other students may lack confidence in their own intellectual judgement. This may spring from broader problems of low self-esteem. Such students may be ill equipped to deal with the robust cut and thrust that is normal in intellectual debate. This may not helped by the fact that fellow PhD students may be among the severest critics. Any PhD student needs to be praised for good work done or interesting insights generated, but particular attention needs to be given to students who may be under-rating themselves. It is important to recognize that there may be a gender dimension in lack of confidence, with some women encountering a chilly or at least insufficiently supportive climate in universities (Tinkler and Jackson, 2004, p. 209).

It may become evident that a particular student is simply not capable of coping with the very special burden of writing a PhD. This is why it is important for departments to have systematic review procedures at least at the end of the first year, with clearly specified requirements that students have to meet. The QAA requires that there should be 'clearly defined mechanisms for formal reviews of student progress, including explicit review stages ... involving individuals independent of the supervisor(s) and the student' (QAA, 2004, p.18). The burden of making a judgement about whether a student should continue is then shared by a group of colleagues who are able to pool their expertise. It is not easy to tell an intellectually ambitious student that he or she is unlikely to achieve his or her cherished goal of completing a PhD. However, it is better for him or her to be told that after one year than to fail to submit after several years of wasted effort and considerable expenditure.

A third pattern of difficulty is the student who is generally promising but has difficulty in putting thoughts into words. As Luke remarked:

> The danger that you need to watch out for is the PhD student who has a pathological fear of writing. You can get into a situation after 18 months or two years where people have effectively written nothing.

PhD students should be encouraged to write from the early stages of the thesis, even if much of what is written is subsequently discarded. Writing helps PhD students to organize their thoughts. It enables them to show that they have understood the relevant literature and clarified their theoretical perspectives. As the thesis progresses, it shows where crucial information is lacking. From the point of view of supervisors, it makes it much easier to offer constructive and specific feedback if they have a piece of written work in front of them. Otherwise supervision sessions can easily become insufficiently focused.

Supervising a PhD student is a demanding role. It can be very wearing if the student is unresponsive to advice or lacks intellectual self-confidence. However, many supervisory relationships work, or can be made to work, very well. Supervising a PhD student can be an enjoyable experience, even if it is time and energy-consuming. What are the factors that lead to a positive and enjoyable relationship? They certainly include basic levels of friendliness and openness and a situation in which the supervision is intellectually interesting and rewarding for the supervisor, reinforcing the earlier point about being selective in accepting PhD students. It is also desirable to establish ground rules at an early stage about what the supervisor can and cannot do, and which tasks are to be seen as the responsibility of the student. 'In the early stages of a supervisory relationship it is very easy to destroy a student's self-confidence by criticism, or to give him or her a false sense of security by too much praise' (Delamont, Atkinson and Parry, 1997, p. 23).

A key part of the role of the supervisor is to act as a motivator. If this is done successfully, the relationship will work better from the perspective of both participants, but it does present particularly difficult challenges. 'PhD students very often go through sloughs of depression about debt and poverty, isolation, thesis problems and poor employment prospects, which the supervisor may be able to alleviate' (Delamont, Atkinson and Parry, 1997, p. 82). To some extent, achieving a PhD is as much a reward for persistence as it is for intellectual talent. Part of the role of the supervisor is to encourage the student to continue in the face of setbacks. Lack and loss of motivation may come from a variety of sources. Apart from financial problems, these may include 'distaste for a particular aspect of the work ... temporary loss of enthusiasm for the whole task ... serious, perhaps clinical, depression' (Delamont, Atkinson and Parry, 1997, p. 93). If the student feels that the supervisor is interested and engaged and encouraging, then it will be easier to handle those difficult but unavoidable conversations when one has to advise a student that a chapter draft or some other piece of work is not up to the required standard. Writing a thesis is ultimately a very lonely task, and at some point the student is likely to become fed up with the topic and discouraged about the possibilities of successful completion. Relatively few students give up, but they may increasingly devote their time to other activities such as teaching, or go off on an intellectual tangent. The task of the supervisor is then to guide them back on course and reinvigorate their enthusiasm for their topic. You may have to do this for someone who irritates you or you have even come to dislike. In other words, successfully supervising a PhD demands the highest standards of professionalism. However, there are few things more satisfying in academic life than seeing an initially unpromising student successfully obtain his or her PhD. It is an activity in which you can make a real and positive difference to someone's life.

▶ Preparing PhD students for examination

The examination of the PhD is the culmination of some four years' work. It is understandably a stressful time for the PhD student. Careful preparation at this stage can assist the chances of a successful outcome. Using empirical research as a basis, this process is treated in much greater depth than is possible here in Tinkler and Jackson (2004). A key decision is the choice of the internal and external examiner. The convention is that the external examiner takes the leading role as the guarantor of standards, but this does not mean that the internal examiner is unimportant. One needs somebody who is familiar with the regulations of the university and the examining process and will also work well with the external examiner. One also needs to avoid anyone who has a reputation as an excessively stringent examiner.

The external examiner has to be reasonably senior and experienced otherwise he or she might not pass the scrutiny tests used at some universities. One rule of thumb that is sometimes used to identify an examiner 'is to give first consideration to the British academic whose work is referenced most frequently in the thesis bibliography' (Burnham, 1997b, p. 194). The professional expertise of the external in the area of the thesis is clearly important, but as suggested in Chapter 2, the value of a very senior individual as a potential referee for the candidate is sometimes exaggerated. Above all, however, one has to pay some attention to the personal qualities and approach to examining of the potential examiner.

At the risk of some caricature, it is possible to divide external examiners into two broad types. One type of examiner looks for signs of originality and value added by the thesis before searching for lines of criticism. This type of examiner generally takes the thesis at face value, that is, he or she does not seek to suggest that the thesis should have approached the topic in a different way, or even that the candidate should have studied something completely different. This type of criticism is particularly difficult for the candidate to deal with, particularly when it is based on personal, political and intellectual agendas (see Tinkler and Jackson, 2004, pp. 70–5). Unfortunately, this is one of the characteristics of the second type of examiner, who sets out to look for flaws in the thesis. Given that no work is perfect, he or she eventually finds a flaw and then uses that as a basis for mounting an onslaught on the thesis. No doubt such examiners would defend themselves by saying that they are taking their gatekeeper role seriously, but the problem is that the gate is set at a different height by different examiners. What this reflects is a broader tension about whether the primary role of the examiner 'is academic community-building or gate-keeping' (Park, 2003, p. 27).

In universities elsewhere in Europe, a somewhat different procedure is used. A panel of examiners (typically between three and five, although there are variations by country) are sent what is effectively a final draft of the thesis. They are invited to state whether or not the thesis is ready for examination or whether some changes are required. This is really the crucial stage of the examination process, and can lead to some vigorous and prolonged debate between the examiners. Once the examiners have agreed that the thesis is ready for defence, an oral examination is held. This is held in public with the family and friends of the candidate usually present. The questioning is generally rigorous and demanding, hence why the room where the candidate waits in one leading Dutch university is known as the 'sweating chamber'. However, it would be unusual for the thesis not to be approved at this stage. The advantage of this approach is that it overcomes the extent to which the UK system is dependent on the potentially unpredictable behaviour of a particular examiner, given that 'it is the external who calls the shots and has the final word on the fate of the thesis' (Burnham, 1997b, p. 194). The downside, just as with panel systems of supervision, is the risk of conflict between the examiners, who may see the occasion as an opportunity to score points off each other. In general, however, examiners behave in a thoroughly professional way.

In any event, the UK system is unlikely to change fundamentally in the foreseeable future, even if it becomes more governed by codes of conduct and the risk of litigation, and innovations such as the appointment of an independent chair to conduct the viva become more common. The choice of the external examiner therefore remains a vital one. Dunleavy (2003, p. 214) provides a description of what a paragon examiner might look like:

> The ideal examiner should have a cheerful personality and strong confidence in herself. She must not feel challenged or threatened by new entrants crowding into her area of expertise, nor affronted by upstart youngsters in the field who take a different view from hers. She should be open to new ideas. She must be able to work constructively with her fellow examiners rather than pursuing hobbyhorses or fixed ideas of her own as if they were all-important. A person of this kind will have a realistic grip on the mechanics of doing research in your discipline.

It would be difficult to find an academic that displayed all those personality traits and skills. As is so often the case, one will usually have to settle for an outcome that is sub-optimal but nevertheless good enough. The key characteristics are a willingness to engage constructively with the thesis, not to be rigid about perspectives and to understand what can reasonably be achieved in four years given that the first year is increasingly taken up with research training. As Luke commented, 'Hopefully a PhD examination should not be an ordeal for anybody, it should be a conversation among relatively equals. A good PhD examination is a rite of passage rather than an inquisition.'

The viva examination

'The research degree viva is one of the most problematic and potentially contentious areas of postgraduate activity' (Park, 2003, p. 24). Park (2003, p. 27) identifies 'four key problems with most current practices relating to doctoral vivas – lack of transparency, the socially constructed nature of the process, the multiple roles expected of the viva, and variability of practice within and between institutions'. From the perspective of the candidate the viva or oral examination is an event surrounded by considerable mystery, reinforced by the folklore that circulates among PhD students. 'The variability of vivas in length, tone and content … contributes to their mystery' (Jackson and Tinkler, 2004, p.14). Doctoral candidates are understandably apprehensive about the viva and one of the tasks of the supervisor is to demystify the event. Providing them with a mock viva a week or two before the actual examination is good practice and gives them some understanding of the likely format to be followed. There are, however, limitations to what can be achieved, given that no two viva examinations are alike. It is not unusual for none of the questions asked in the mock viva to be asked at the real event. This reflects the extent to which 'the viva is a process of engagement in which multiple agendas are at work and the rules are more implicit than explicit and are only vaguely defined' (Park, 2003, p. 27).

Candidates also needed to be reminded that the viva is rarely crucial in determining the outcome of the examination. The examiners will usually have formed a view before the examination about whether the thesis should pass (usually with some minor corrections) or whether it should be referred for further work. If they have decided that the thesis has such serious defects that it needs to be at least partially rewritten, they are unlikely to be deflected from that view by the viva. Occasionally, the candidate is able to mount such a robust defence that they are reassured. What is more likely is that the candidate will be able to reassure them about some of the points that concerned them so that the extent of the work required may be reduced. When the examiners are satisfied that the thesis should pass, the viva performs the function of ensuring that the work is that of the candidate and also of offering some suggestions for developing the work for publication. Very occasionally a candidate who has written a good thesis will perform in a very unsatisfactory way in the viva, for example, a candidate is obstreperous and refuses to answer questions he or she regards as being outside the scope of the thesis. A viva performance that is well below the quality of the thesis places examiners in a difficult situation. Provided that they are satisfied that the thesis is the candidate's own work and that he or she has a familiarity with the general subject area, they are unlikely to refer the thesis on the basis of the viva performance if the thesis itself is a good one. Apart from anything else, it would be difficult to specify the basis for a referral. If you have a candidate who is short-tempered or difficult, try to emphasize to him or her the importance of being pleasant and cooperative with the examiners.

Referral

Few theses are passed without the requirement for minor corrections. Many universities also have a procedure that allows a period of one to three months for minor substantive corrections that go beyond shortcomings in presentation. However, some theses are referred: that is to say, the examiners specify a list of major changes that they require to be made to the thesis. The thesis then has to resubmitted after a specified time period, which can vary according to the extent of the changes required and the circumstances of the candidate, but might be six or 12 months. There cannot be a further referral as the examiners have to make a decision about whether to pass the resubmitted thesis, award an MPhil degree or, exceptionally, fail it altogether. It is unusual for there to be a second viva following a referral.

Referral is a difficult situation for the supervisor and the student and needs to be handled with particular care. 'Referral is often seen by research students as complete failure' (Dunleavy, 2003, p. 221). The candidate may have been looking forward to the period beyond the thesis, to writing up for publication and getting on with the next stage of his or her life. Suddenly he or she is faced with a period of additional work and continuing uncertainty, although referred theses are passed if the conditions laid down by the examiners are met. If the candidate does not have a job, he or she might be concerned that the chances of obtaining one have been affected. If the person already has a job, it is not easy to make the changes to the thesis while coping with the demands of a new post.

The role of the supervisor in such circumstances must focus on providing reassurance to the candidate. Dunleavy (2003, p. 225) suggests that 'The supervisor's role is ... crucial after a referral, in ensuring that you are asked only for a clear and achievable set of changes.' It is important that the examiners specify clearly what is required: a failure to do so properly can lead to appeals. However, the examiners may consider that their independence is undermined if the supervisor attempts to intervene too much, and it could even be counterproductive.

In very broad terms, students may react in two ways to referrals: depression or aggression. In the more depressive reactions, students may blame themselves for what they see as their own inadequacies. Very often they focus on their performance in the viva, but as noted earlier, the viva is rarely crucial in determining the outcome of the examination. This needs to be pointed out to the student, otherwise he or she will be constantly agonizing about the way in which he or she answered particular questions. Student needs to be reassured that their work is essentially sound (and good examiners will have complemented them on the strong points) but needs to be strengthened in certain ways to produce a better thesis. Students should be advised that the work can readily be undertaken providing they follow the advice of the examiners. There is usually a few weeks before the official communication from the university arrives, giving them time to recuperate.

Some students may react in a more aggressive way; indeed an aggressive phase may follow a depressive one. They may express dissatisfaction with the examiners, bring parents from abroad to remonstrate (it does happen), or blame the supervisor on the lines of 'my failure is your failure'. This is one situation where it helps to have more than one supervisor. To some extent, however, you simply have to listen to what is said, which can help the storm to blow over.

Some students will inevitably think about appeals. This is really only appropriate at this stage in the case of the award of an MPhil or an outright failure. Appeals against PhD decisions are rarely successful, and when they are, it is usually on procedural grounds: for example, the viva examination was not conducted properly or the candidate was not given sufficiently clear and explicit guidance on the changes required in a referred thesis. 'It is worth noting that candidates may not challenge the academic judgement of the examiners' (Tinkler and Jackson, 2004, p. 214). Complaints that supervision was inadequate are unlikely to succeed (or may even not be allowed) if no complaint was made about the quality of the supervision before the examination. (It is a different matter if there are no adequate mechanisms for making or dealing with such complaints or they are disregarded.) Given that universities scrutinize the credentials of examiners, it is difficult to establish that they are incompetent or have acted with bias against a candidate. Universities are unlikely to be sympathetic to appeals that essentially ask for a different set of examiners to be appointed to produce the right result, although new examiners can be appointed where there have been procedural failures. Universities do have an important gatekeeper function in relation to the award of PhDs and would be open to criticism if standards were unduly relaxed.

PhD supervision is a very demanding role that calls on a considerable range of qualities, not just professional knowledge and expertise, but also the need to develop a relationship with the doctoral student that is mutually satisfactory for both parties. You need to secure the confidence of students so that they will accept your guidance, but avoid a situation in which they become over-reliant on you. If this occurs, they will not develop their own intellectual autonomy and distinctive position and are likely to make excessive demands on your time and even your emotional resilience. One of the difficulties that have to be recognized is that PhD students talk a lot among themselves, which is very desirable as it is part of the development of an intellectual community and networks of mutual support that can often last a lifetime. However, these discussions can also lead to the development of a strong folklore and misleading myths about the nature of what is still a somewhat idiosyncratic process of academic apprenticeship. Research training should help to dispel some of these myths, but there is still an important role for the supervisor as an intellectual and procedural guide.

▶ Examining PhDs

Being invited to examine a PhD is another milestone on the road to becoming a successful and established academic. Just as with supervision, however, a cautious approach is necessary. Of course, the commitment is a much more limited one in duration: several days' work on the thesis and a visit to the university where the candidate is located. Nevertheless, it can be quite a wearing experience. As Luke commented:

> Reading a PhD is a pain, especially if it's plodding. PhDs don't tend to be great literature: they tend to be plodding, they tend to be methodical, they tend to be worthy, they tend to be dull.

Although the fees paid to external examiners have improved somewhat, they bear no relationship to the amount of work put in, reflecting the fact that doctoral (like external) examining is seen primarily as a professional obligation. It is interesting to speculate whether doctors or lawyers would undertake a professional obligation at below the market rate. If you are the internal examiner, you will probably be paid less than the external and perhaps nothing at all, and you will have the responsibility of organizing the examination and looking after the external examiner. In particular it is important that you are familiar with the rules of your university and how they should be applied in difficult cases. (If there is any uncertainty you can ring your graduate office for advice.) If the candidate is referred, be aware that he or she may turn to you for advice in the redrafting process. Although it is reasonable to clarify particular points about which the candidate is uncertain, you should not get into long discussions or email exchanges with him or her. The primary responsibility remains with the supervisor, and you should point the candidate in that direction.

As far as invitations to examine abroad are concerned, these are usually worth accepting. You will be a member of a panel, so your responsibility is shared. Payment for your services is at a much higher rate than in the UK, and there is the added bonus of an expenses-paid trip abroad, possibly to an attractive destination such as Florence or Barcelona. However, this is not an opportunity for intellectual tourism with some light examining duties thrown in. Drawing on her experience of examining abroad, Lauren cautioned:

> The thesis still needs to be read, you personally will still be required to pursue a line of questioning at some length, you will still be an essential part of the decision-making process (even though the responsibility is shared between more people), you will still be required to correspond and interact with the student should any problems arise and the thesis be referred for any reason (though in other systems this is less common) and so on. In addition, you will need to acquaint yourself with a different system beforehand and become familiar with the rules and procedures in this system, which can be very time-consuming. In short, I don't think there is less work involved (and, in some respects, quite the opposite).

How should you prepare for your first doctoral examination? Try to set aside blocks of time in a location free from interruption to work on the thesis. Read the thesis carefully, making notes about potential problems and possible questions, but also highlighting areas of strength. Keep a separate sheet of paper or a computer file for typos and grammatical and spelling errors, as the candidate will need to be handed a list of required corrections. You also need to be alert to the possibility of plagiarism, which unfortunately is not unknown in PhDs. Once the process of reading is complete, prepare a statement of major and minor issues that you would like to raise in the viva. This can also provide the basis of your preliminary report, if one is required. Prepare your list of questions for the viva, which should attempt to synthesize the main points for discussion rather than go through the thesis page by page. Clearly many of the questions will relate to the particular content of the thesis, but, as Luke pointed out, 'A lot of the questions I'll ask in different PhD exams are effectively the same question. There are certain questions about case selection, about methodology, about theory that are pretty common to all PhDs.'

As has been noted earlier in the chapter, procedures in relation to PhDs are less standardized than other aspects of university business. The areas in which procedures may differ including the following:

- Whether examiners are required to exchange preliminary reports before the examination (these also usually have to be forwarded to the university after the examination). This does represent a helpful practice because it allows the examiners to see whether their independent scrutiny of the thesis has raised similar questions and helps them to think about the viva more effectively in advance, rather than having a rushed conversation over lunch before the examination. Even if preliminary reports are required, it might be sensible to follow Luke's advice and 'have a conversation prior to the day just to get a basic ball park sense of what we're thinking about'.
- Whether there are any specific dress requirements for the examination. Oxford University would probably not insist on examiners from outside the university wearing subfusc, but if the student has had to parade through the town in gown and bow tie and be photographed by tourists, it might be a courtesy to be similarly attired.
- Whether the examination is held in public. In most universities it is not, and even where it is, there is rarely an audience.
- Whether the supervisor is permitted to be present in the examination and whether he or she will be a silent observer or can participate either with or without invitation (see Tinkler and Jackson, 2004, p. 84). Even if this is permitted, it is probably not good practice, as it tends to unsettle both the student and the examiners.

At all universities, the examiners' decision constitutes a recommendation that has to be confirmed by the senate. (What usually happens is that a dean of graduate studies scrutinizes the reports.) Nevertheless, it is usual to convey the recommendation to the candidate at the time of the viva. This will be an easy task if the candidate is successful. If the thesis has been referred, the candidate may be upset and it is best not to get into a lengthy conversation with either the candidate or the supervisor about the reasons for the decision. Emphasize that a detailed report will be made available, stating what changes need to be made to the thesis. It is important that this report is precise and detailed, otherwise it is difficult for the candidate to know exactly what is required, and the whole matter may end up in an appeals process.

▶ Conclusions

The nature of supervision of research theses is changing, with greater emphasis on systematic research training before undertaking the thesis in a 1+3 model and the more frequent provision of more than one supervisor. However, the contribution of second supervisors may often be purely nominal, allowing the department to check a box stating that more than one supervisor has been provided. Considerable responsibility is still placed on the lead or main supervisor. The sense of responsibility can lead to the risk of getting too close to the student or the relationship becoming too personal. The relationship is always going to be asymmetrical to some extent, but if students become too dependent on their supervisors, they are less likely to develop successfully into mature and independent academics. They may also place excessive demands on the supervisor's time. One needs to be engaged with students and professionally concerned with them, but it is also important to maintain a certain intellectual distance.

Many academics who have never supervised a PhD student or examined one would doubtless like to be in a situation where they could. This chapter has emphasized some of the demands and responsibilities associated with PhD supervision and examination. Nevertheless, it is also a form of academic work that can be intellectually rewarding and personally satisfying. It has been necessary to point out some of the pitfalls and the ways in which things can go wrong, but the majority of PhD supervisions work smoothly and successfully. Supervision should be sought rather than avoided, but alongside a realistic appreciation of what is involved.

6 Getting Published

This chapter deals with how you can get your research work published. The first part of the chapter deals with the context provided by the RAE, which generates considerable pressure to publish, particularly in the more research-oriented universities. Even academics in universities that emphasize teaching may still wish to publish, in order to advance their careers or simply to transmit their ideas to a wider audience. 'Publish or perish' was not, of course, a slogan invented for the RAE, but systematic research assessment has had a considerable impact on the form in which publication occurs. The second part of the chapter sets out to review the merits of the various forms of publication from academic monographs to websites, including advice about what to do about publishing your PhD as a book. It concludes with a discussion of the advantages and disadvantages of co-authorship. The third section deals with the mechanics of publication, ranging from working with copy editors to producing an index. Finally, the conclusion discusses some possible longer-term trends in academic publishing.

▶ The RAE context

Any discussion of getting published has to take account of the context provided by the RAE process and also by the shift towards full economic costing of research grants within the dual funding system. The way in which research and publishing is undertaken by an academic at an early stage of a career will be influenced by the pressures from departments anxious to make the best possible submission to the 2008 RAE. If an academic is located in a department that is not going to make an RAE submission, the wish to switch to a more research-oriented department may still influence his or her writing strategy.

The RAE is a highly controversial subject in academic life. Many academics consider that it has changed academic life irretrievably for the worse. In making any evaluation of the RAE, it is necessary to distinguish between the principle of having such an evaluation at all; the way it has been conducted; and the financial decisions that have been taken on the basis of the RAE outcome.

The need for some assessment of the research undertaken in universities arises from the fact that if most institutions are receiving public funding to undertake research, there needs to be a mechanism to ensure that the money is being spent for the purpose that it was intended and that it leads to work that advances knowledge. When there was no RAE, and scrutiny was limited to occasional 'visitations' from the old University Grants Committee (UGC), it was possible for many members of a university to be undertaking very little research or none at all. Indeed, research-inactive members of a department were not only receiving research support but not making use of it, they also often acted as a block to younger members of a department whose research activity was seen as a threat to them and a form of 'rate busting'. One consequence of the introduction of the RAE system, which started with the Research Selectivity Exercise conducted by the UGC in 1986, is that this type of attitude can no longer be sustained. It has also opened up more varied and rapid promotion opportunities for younger, research-active scholars. It is all too easy to think of a past golden age in universities when there was leisure to undertake serious scholarship without also reflecting about the conservatism this often encouraged. All too often, assessments of the RAE focus on the costs and not on the benefits. The Higher Education Funding Council for England's (HEFCE) view of the benefits of the RAE is set out in Box 6.1, along with some common criticisms.

There is no doubt that the RAE places considerable pressures on young researchers. Ruth commented that a major challenge was 'the RAE, and this whole drive to produce outputs, churn out the work, which diminishes the pleasure in doing the work in the first place'. Lauren noted that:

> There are huge challenges associated with fitting into a RAE driven culture and how to manage the trade offs that that does sometimes represent with intellectual endeavours. There is such a pressure on output that it is difficult to convince yourself to slow down and take your time with a particular piece.

Some young academics may leave academic life as a consequence or 'burn out' at an early stage in their career. It may lead young academics to 'play safe' and write a series of articles that are safely within the

---

Box 6.1 HEFCE's view of the RAE

The RAE is generally agreed to have had a significant positive impact. The exercise has driven a substantial improvement in the overall quality of the UK research base, and has made a major contribution to maintaining national economic growth and international competitiveness. It has highlighted the very best research and has encouraged higher education institutes (HEIs) to take a rigorous approach in developing and implementing their own research strategies. It has enabled the government and funding bodies to maximise the return from the limited public funds available for basic research. The RAE has also strengthened the dual support system for research funding – under which grant from the funding bodies supports a permanent research capability and infrastructure, and basic curiosity-driven research – underpinning the higher education sector's capacity to undertake research of public benefit commissioned by the research councils, charities and others.

At the same time, the exercise has been subject to some criticism. Concerns have been expressed that the exercise:

- favours established disciplines and approaches over new and inter-disciplinary work
- does not deal well with applied and practice-based research in particular
- places an undue administrative burden on the sector
- has a negative impact upon institutional behaviour as HEIs and departments manage their research strategies, and shape their RAE submissions, in order to achieve the highest possible ratings.

Source: RAE (2004), p. 4.

---

mainstream of their discipline rather than an in-depth research monograph that will challenge prevailing orthodoxies. Mark commented:

> The thing is that the RAE pressures and the current environment actually militate against individuals taking risks in their writing. It is easy to regurgitate what you have done and maybe add a few more sentences or thoughts ... The rational actor simply plays safe and continues to write coherent but not terribly challenging articles.

From this perspective, the RAE fails to meet one of its key principles:

> Developing an assessment process which operates neutrally without distorting the activity that it measures and neither encourages nor discourages any particular type of activity or behaviour other than providing a stimulus to the improvement of research quality overall.

(RAE, 2005, p. 2)

One of the concerns that academics in the humanities and social sciences have had about the RAE was that it was largely driven by a need to solve problems in the natural sciences. Much natural science research is capital-intensive, demanding purpose-built laboratories and expensive capital equipment. There is therefore a case for concentrating research at a relatively small number of locations, which does not apply in the same way in the humanities and social sciences, notwithstanding the advantages of people working together in a research group at the same location. These concerns were intensified by the funding decisions taken after the 2001 RAE. Departments graded as 3A had their research funding eliminated, and Grade 4 departments (accounting for 25 per cent of research-active staff), which had supposedly attained national standing with some evidence of international excellence, had their research funding cut by 42 per cent. This reflected a government higher education policy that was informed by 'a belief that benefits will come from concentrating research in larger units' (Evidence, 2003, p. 7). In part, this seemed to rely on confusion between the benefits of selectivity and concentration. There 'is no general evidence to support the widely held supposition that bigger units necessarily do better research' (Evidence, 2003, p. 25).

The 2008 RAE

In developing their proposals for the RAE to be completed in 2008, the funding councils sought to respond to criticisms of earlier exercises, in particular variability between the decisions taken by different disciplinary panels. A new system of main panels and sub-panels was developed, with the sub-panels being concerned with particular or closely related disciplines, and the main panels covering groups of disciplines, the grouping of which was not without controversy. The main panels will oversee the criteria and working methods of the sub-panels and will take the final rating decisions, but on the basis of recommendations of the sub-panels who will still undertake the greater part of the work of assessing returns, reading publications and making rating decisions.

From the point of view of policy makers, with over half of all work submitted graded as either 5 or 5*, the 2001 RAE had failed to provide 'the degree of discrimination required by a policy of selective funding' (RAE, 2004, p. 4). The rating scale was therefore replaced by a quality profile in which three of the four categories require work of international quality. In other words, the bar has been raised higher than in early exercises to ensure that a concentration of funds in units deemed excellent continues. A sample quality profile provided by the funding councils is reproduced in Table 6.1. Although the figures are stated to be for fictional universities, university X might represent a successful research university and university Y a post-1992 university.

Quality levels are defined in terms of the following categories (RAE, 2005, p. 24):

- Four star. Quality that is world-leading in terms of originality, significance and rigour. This standard will be achieved by a research output that is, or is likely to become, a primary reference point of the field or sub-field. (This is sometimes colloquially referred to as the 'Einstein' or 'Nobel prize' criterion, and it was suggested that it is likely to be fulfilled by only a few works. Indications from the sub-panels are that attaining this standard will not be as impossibly hard as these comments suggested. Work that changes how we think about a particular aspect of a discipline should qualify.)
- Three star. Quality that is internationally excellent in terms of originality, significance and rigour, but nonetheless falls short of the

Table 6.1 Sample quality profile for two units of assessment

% of research activity meeting standard for	University X	University Y
4 star	15	0
3 star	25	5
2 star	40	40
1 star	15	45
Unclassified	5	10

Source: RAE (2005), p. 24.

highest standards of excellence. This standard will be achieved by a research output that is, or is likely to become, a major reference point that substantially advances knowledge and understanding of the field or sub-field.

- Two star. Quality that is recognized internationally in terms of originality, significance and rigour. This standard will be achieved by a research output that is, or is likely to become, a reference point that advances knowledge and understanding of the field or sub-field. (The distinction between three star and two star is a crucial one that panels will frequently have to make, but it will not be easy to distinguish between 'internationally excellent' and 'recognized internationally' even with the use of the words 'major' and 'substantially' as differentiators.)
- One star. Quality that is recognized nationally in terms of originality, significance and rigour. This standard will be achieved by a research output that makes, or is likely to make, a contribution to knowledge or understanding of the field or sub-field.
- Unclassified. Quality that falls below the standard of nationally recognized work, or work that does not meet the published definition of research for the purposes of assessment.

The quality profile will be made up of three main components: research outputs (not less than 50 per cent of the total); research environment (not less than 5 per cent of the total); and esteem indicators (not less than 5 per cent of the total). The actual weighting given to each of these components was decided by the main panels, some following the illustrative example provided by the funding councils that gave a 70 per cent weighting to research outputs, a 20 per cent weighting to research environment and a 10 per cent weighting to esteem indicators (RAE, 2005, p. 25). In the social sciences, three out of the four main panels gave a 75 per cent weighting to outputs, although this was reduced to 70 per cent for the sub-panel covering business and management studies. In the arts and humanities, the output weighting was as high as 80 per cent in Panel N covering subjects such as history, philosophy and theology, but 70 per cent for the area studies panel, which gave a particularly high rating to esteem (15 per cent).

The main pressure on young researchers will thus be in terms of research outputs, in part because this measure will have the greatest weight in the eventual outcome. Research income, students and studentships as well as textual information on research strategy, environment and esteem will formally factor into the quality profile for each submission. They will 'count for cash' and may have a substantial influence on the overall quality profile outcome. However, this aspect of the exercise will be relatively remote from new entrants. They will not be required to draft the textual commentary on the research environment. As far as esteem indicators are concerned, however, these apply to a department as a collectivity, so sub-panels can be expected to look for departments where everyone is doing interesting and worthwhile things. Attention will also be paid to new entrants as the object of 'strategies for promoting and developing research staff ('particularly those new to research') (RAE, 2005, p.15).

Young researchers will therefore often be under pressure to provide four research outputs that will be ready in good time for the submission date. (The timetable for the 2008 RAE is summarized in Table 6.2.) This is notwithstanding the fact that sub-panels are enjoined to 'Take account of the situation of early career researchers' who will 'automatically be flagged in submissions' (RAE, 2005, p. 13). Their date of entry into the profession will be returned, although this does involve some complications about how one calculates a date of entry (technically viewed as eligibility for a Category A submission). Persons appointed to their first full-time post after 1 August 2003 will be treated as early career researchers, and the expectation is that a person appointed between then and 1 August 2005 would contribute two outputs. Anyone appointed after 1 August 2005 would only be expected to contribute one output.

The choice of RAE outputs

The exact mix of outputs will vary somewhat from discipline to discipline. In some branches of the humanities research outputs may

Table 6.2 Timetable for the 2008 RAE	
By 31 December 2005	Final criteria and working methods of panels and sub-panels issued (slightly delayed)
31 October 2007	Census date
30 November 2007	Final date for submissions
31 December 2007	Cut-off point for publication of research outputs
January–November 2008	Assessment phase
December 2008	Results published

include, for example, images, buildings, performances, exhibits or events, and work published in non-print media (RAE, 2005, p. 13). Between disciplines where output is very largely confined to print media, the weight given to various forms of publication may vary. The draft criteria issued by sub-panels for the 2008 exercise contain statements such as that made by the politics and international relations sub-panel, 'All forms of research output will be treated equally. The sub-panel will not rank or regard any particular form of output as of greater or lesser quality than another *per se*.' Economics as a discipline has given a very substantial weight to refereed journal articles in key journals, but its sub-panel states that it 'will not regard any type of output as inherently being of higher quality than another'. Nevertheless, academics suspect that panel members may be subtly influenced by the wrapping as well as its content, and will be initially impressed by something that appears in a highly regarded journal, even though leading journals sometimes fail to meet their own standards. Disciplines in the humanities look more favourably on research monographs, so that in many disciplines a 'gold standard' might be seen as consisting of a research monograph and three refereed journal articles in highly regarded journals. Panels in the humanities have made provision for so-called 'super books', which in some cases will count as the equivalent of two outputs, but may count for even more.

University departments will not wish to submit textbooks, although a complicating factor is the practice of some publishers of attempting to market as textbooks what are in fact research monographs, a problem that is specifically recognized by the politics and international relations sub-panel. Books that contain original research as well as a synthesis of earlier research may legitimately serve as texts for advanced courses and also be entered in the RAE. Book chapters are unlikely to be looked on favourably by departments, as they have not gone through rigorous peer review processes, even if they might make a greater contribution to the discipline than many journal articles. This is particularly unfortunate for a number of reasons. First, 'the absence of [peer] review may not, in itself, be taken to imply lower quality' (RAE, 2005, p. 14). Second, although it may not be possible to read all submitted outputs, and in practice outputs are likely to be read sufficiently to reach a judgement about their professional standing, there will be quite extensive reading. Third, in the 2001 RAE, there is some evidence that even highly rated departments did not confine themselves to research monographs or refereed journal articles.

▶ Different forms of publication: academic monographs and textbooks

Academics can choose between various different forms of publication of their ideas. In some cases the choices made will be influenced by disciplinary preferences: for example, the emphasis placed on refereed journal articles above everything else in economics. Disciplinary norms aside, most academics will use a mixture of forms of publication. Often this reflects opportunities for publication that are offered to you: for example, after presenting a conference paper you are invited to contribute a chapter to an edited book. You should not, however, accept all the publication opportunities that are presented to you without reflection. Time management has to be taken into account, and in particular the way in which a small-scale project such as a book chapter which looks as if it could be completed relatively quickly delays work of greater importance in the long term.

In most of the disciplines covered in this book, failure to produce a research monograph after a number of years could well count against someone who has a good portfolio of refereed journal articles. A good research monograph is seen as evidence of your ability to write about a problem in depth and hence to make a distinctive contribution to your discipline. Writing such a book represents a major commitment that is likely to extend over a number of years. Nevertheless, books have some advantages over journal articles, particularly in terms of their impact. As Dunleavy (2003, p. 252) notes, 'A book, any book, is a surprisingly long-lived and multi-accessible artefact ... Books are usually much more cited than journal articles.' Nevertheless, writing a book is not an easy option. Ruth commented:

> I went through absolute hell. It came out three years ago and I'm still getting over it. It's only now that I'm contemplating writing another and because it has been pointed out to me that I need to do so.

Textbooks

The distinction between a research monograph and a textbook is not always a clear one. In part this is because some publishers like to market what are in fact research monographs as if they were textbooks. Of course, the two functions can be combined. A research monograph may also serve as a core reader for an advanced undergraduate option or MA module. However, one has to be careful about a publisher pressurizing you to make your book less like a research monograph and more like a textbook. As Luke recalled:

> Publishers want to publish textbooks. There is a space between what the publisher thinks and what you think, you can present what the publisher thinks is a textbook as a monograph. I think that circle can be squared. I did need to open that space because there was a definite pressure from the publisher to make [Luke's book] more textbooky, to give it the cosmetic feel of being a textbook.

Publisher Steven Kennedy has written a defence of the academic textbook in the context of the pressures generated by the RAE. He argues that textbooks are not useful just as a means of introducing students to a subject and making cutting-edge research accessible to them. In his view:

> [Textbooks] play a crucial role in systematising fragmented research findings and disparate debates to communicate them to a wider audience … They are … a crucial link in the chain of academic progress by establishing baselines for researchers in an ever-more specialised world.
>
> (Kennedy, 2004)

There is much in Kennedy's argument that 'The analytical and research skills involved in writing such texts are much underrated' and that the treatment of textbooks represents an example of the RAE emphasizing measurable rather than desirable outputs. Teaching would become very difficult if the supply of good textbooks dried up. Web-based resources are not an adequate substitute because they do not provide students with guidance and structure. However, new entrants to an academic career cannot alter the context in which they work in the short to medium term. Devoting the considerable effort required to produce a successful textbook would not provide a good beginning to their career.

Textbooks may be more time-consuming and difficult to write than monographs. Drawing on his extensive experience as a monograph and textbook writer, Moran (2005, p. 4) notes, 'the student text was much the more difficult to write'. The textbook was more rigorously refereed and he had to write about areas where he had no record of specialized research. He also had to address a variety of audiences, beginners who would use the book and peers who need to be persuaded to recommend it. 'The easiest part of the process was writing the words. The really tricky part was composing the accompaniment: photos, documents, briefing boxes, timelines, debates and issue boxes, cartoons, and so on' (Moran, 2005, p. 4).

Textbooks do, of course, generate substantially more income in the form of royalties than research monographs which, if they yield any financial return at all, will usually only produce a three-figure sum. A textbook that is sold into schools could well generate five-figure sales and an equivalent sum in royalties, and that can apply to some very successful first-year undergraduate textbooks. However, those sums have to be set against the financial gains arising from earlier promotion or securing a permanent post. Moreover, textbooks involve a substantial continuing commitment, as they require frequent revision to keep up to date, and increasingly are accompanied by websites which also require maintenance and updating. Of course, academics are not generally writing for money but to secure a wider audience for their ideas.

In any case, younger academics are not generally approached to write textbooks, as they require the knowledge and understanding of a broad field that is generally acquired later in a career. The 'name' or reputation of a senior academic may help to sell the book. Younger academics may, however, sometimes be asked to write a short survey of an emerging field in which they are expert or even an introduction to a particular concept. An option of this kind may be worth considering as it may offer 'the best of all worlds'. It may enhance your reputation as someone who has a good understanding of a new field. As such books are relatively short they will not take as long to write as a full research monograph. They may also make you some money, which is a consideration when you still have an overhang of debt from your days as a student. Once again, however, it is important to ensure that the publisher does not push you too far in the direction of a textbook format. A pocket-sized physical format may also attract slighting comments. A book of this kind needs to be more than a systematic survey of a field, but also a venue in which you provide original and challenging insights. In that format, it will also be acceptable as a RAE contribution.

Choosing a publisher

The economic environment for publishing academic research monographs has become increasingly difficult. Publishers are finding that financially hard-pressed students are confining purchases to one or at most two textbooks for each course, many of which can be found on the second-hand market. Sales of supplementary books for modules have been in a rapid decline. Students are reluctant to buy anything beyond the core textbook for their course. This means that most research monographs rely on library sales. It is in fact still possible to make a profit on a book that sells only 300 copies, primarily library copies, but this usually means a price in the £50–60 range. This does not mean that publishers are indifferent to the size of the market for books of this type. They still want to be reassured that the book is of a high academic standard and the material cutting-edge or innovative so that it will attract favourable reviews. They will want to be reassured that the author is a recognized or at least emergent expert in the area, and that the book has some potential for international sales, particularly in the United States. Having crossed all these hurdles, the high price may mean that fewer people than you would like to might therefore get to read your book, but this may not diminish its value for RAE or promotion purposes.

One result of the difficult economic climate in publishing has been that 'as the academic publishing industry has been consolidated into larger and more commercially orientated global corporations, the number of major firms that actually handle academic monographs has sharply declined since the 1980s' (Dunleavy, 2003, p. 252). A consequence is that publishers place an increasing emphasis on journal publishing, which is seen as more lucrative. Broadly speaking, the book publishers can be divided into four main categories: the major university presses, both here and in the United States; major commercial publishers; smaller-scale commercial publishers; and publishers that are sometimes portrayed as 'academic vanity presses'. Each of these types of publisher has its advantages and disadvantages. It is important to invest some effort in understanding the nature of publishing and the constraints under which it operates, as Emma learnt:

> It is getting to understand what academic publishing is like and what the publishers are looking for. It is an enterprise in itself. Learning all about commercial publishing is important, I don't think anybody ever warned me about that.

You will achieve considerable prestige if you succeed in publishing with one of the major university presses, Oxford University Press or Cambridge University Press. This is not an impossible target for a young researcher, as some of our respondents were publishing with these prestigious presses. Manchester University Press also enjoys a good reputation, but is not seen as being quite in the same league, particularly in terms of presence outside the UK, while Edinburgh University Press has an emphasis on books with a Scottish content or theme and seeks to be the leading publisher of serious books about Scotland. There are also some very highly regarded US university presses such as Harvard and Princeton, but the difficulties of publishing with the Oxbridge presses discussed below are probably compounded for them. It may, however, be an option worth considering if you have a book manuscript in an area such as US history, literature, film or politics.

To succeed with Oxford and Cambridge university presses, you will need a book of very high quality and you should expect the scrutiny process to be more rigorous and prolonged than with other publishers. This does not mean, however, that it is not a viable option for younger academics, but you will need to persevere. Lucy's experience is relevant in this respect:

> [Andrew] and I, who are writing a joint book together, really wanted it to be with a very good publisher. We spent a lot of time doing research about marketing it and who would read it and why. He did that side it of it and I wrote the sample chapter and made it very tight. And then we were able to get a contract with Oxford University Press, which is what we really wanted. It took a long time and it was very difficult and they asked for another draft of the sample chapter and another draft of the plan. I suppose it's just kind of keeping going with it really.

Major commercial publishers are perfectly reputable outlets for a book. They may not as have as much prestige as the major university presses but they are still well regarded. Their books are usually put through a peer review process. They do, however, tend to be major textbook publishers and there is always the risk that they will try to push your book in a textbook direction. Because they publish large numbers of titles, your book will be to some extent lost in a very large catalogue. Many of their books are published in series on particular themes, and it is worth carrying out some research to see if there is a series that fits your particular title. Many series are quite broad in their definitions and quite elastic in their application. There is more of an academic input to the selection of titles, as the series editor(s) are usually senior academics. They want more high-quality titles for their series and they are usually keen to help younger academics. It is worth noting, however, that a series can acquire a positive or a negative reputation.

If a series accepts too many titles so that it loses focus and seems to lack discernment, it may no longer be a good place to publish.

Smaller-scale commercial publishers can be good outlets for a book from a young academic. In general, they are distinguished from larger commercial publishers in terms of not engaging in textbook publication, but concentrating on academic monographs. Some of them may have quite long lists, but concentrated on a few disciplines: for example Edward Elgar, which has a social science focus and is particularly strong in economics and environmental studies (www.e-elgar.co.uk). They are less likely to cross the border between the humanities and the social sciences than larger-scale publishers, although I. B. Tauris is an interesting if rare example of an independent publishing house that publishes 175 books a year in the humanities and social sciences (http://www.ibtauris.com/).

These smaller publishers still need to make a profit out of your book, but are generally more comfortable with books that are unlikely to achieve large sales. However, in part they cope with this by paring down production costs. They may expect you to produce camera-ready copy from a laser printer. The standard of finish is quite acceptable, but the process of production, for example keeping your printed copy within the required page margins, can be quite fiddly and time-consuming. They may also send out fewer review copies than other publishers to try to avoid a situation where they give away 100 copies of a book that sells 300. However, this is unlikely to have much impact on the chances of your book being reviewed, as academic books sent to general weeklies like the *Economist*, *Spectator*, *Prospect* and so on rarely get reviewed.

A vanity press is a commercial enterprise that charges authors for publication, either all or some of the full economic cost. In return the author receives a number of copies free of charge. They are often used for publishing family histories, autobiographies by people of no special distinction or books on obscure hobbies. Obviously academics should stay well away from them. However, there are some academic publishers that are regarded as low-prestige outlets and have been known to be referred to as 'academic vanity presses'. This is a misnomer as they do not charge for publication, although they may not pay any royalties. It is also unfair in the sense that they often produce books which are highly specialized but nevertheless of good academic quality. However, if you do publish with them, your book may be less well regarded than if it was published elsewhere, regardless of its intrinsic quality. It is important to research prospective publishers by looking at their websites and catalogues and by talking about their reputation to more senior colleagues.

Approaching a publisher

One key piece of advice is that you should not write a book before trying to find a publisher. You may then find that no one is interested in the book because it is not commercially viable and you have wasted a great deal of time. Publishers will not want to see a completed manuscript before they make a decision about whether to publish a book (or if any offer is deferred until such a manuscript is produced, it suggests that they have serious reservations about publication). Although you may be fortunate in being identified as a rising star, with Ann being approached by Cambridge University Press, finding a publisher is not generally easy and may take some time. As Ruth commented, 'I was prepared for it to be a difficult process.'

Often opportunities arise to have informal discussions with publishers or series editors at conferences, and these are well worth taking. Lucy's first book was in 'a series that was edited by a professor I met at a conference and I talked to her about the project and she said "That sounds as if it would fit into a series, why don't you give it to us?"' It is possible that someone in your department or university may edit a relevant book series. Very often, however, finding a publisher will involve a form of 'cold calling'. Usually publishers will provide guidance on their websites detailing the information they require from prospective authors. Requirements will vary somewhat from one publisher to another, but usually they will want an outline plan of the book, a sample chapter or chapters, and a completed form that gives information on a number of subjects but particularly the market potential for the book. In putting together these materials, it is important to strike a balance between emphasizing what is distinctive about the book and over-selling it. Exaggerated claims about likely sales will not be regarded with any credibility by the publisher. If there are particular markets in which the book is likely to sell well, be as specific about them as possible, as well as about the distinctive academic merits of the book. In the humanities, centenaries (births, deaths or publication of a particular book) may provide a good peg on which to hang a monograph.

The material you have submitted will usually be sent within the publishers to the commissioning editor for your discipline or specialist area, and to the academic series editor if there is one. Sometimes the commissioning editor will be responsible for more than one discipline, depending on how large the publisher is and its internal organization. Commissioning editors in the major university presses may have less autonomy, with final decisions taken by a supervising committee. In general, however, commissioning editors are very knowledgeable about the disciplines in which they operate. Indeed, they probably know more about what is happening in the discipline than many academics, and are often key figures within it. An understanding of new developments and trends within the discipline is part of their stock in trade.

If the commissioning editor thinks that the book has a reasonable chance of academic and commercial success, it will be sent to two or more reviewers for their opinions. These reviewers are usually relatively senior academics in the discipline. (In the case of a series one of the editors will normally act as a reviewer.) The publisher will provide them with a standard list of questions to answer about the book, but may also indicate particular concerns that he she has or points that should be addressed in the report.

Quite often, commissioning editors give an indication of the kind of response they would like to receive: for example, they hint that they are enthusiastic about the book and would welcome a positive endorsement for their own internal use. Although the reviewers will address the academic strengths and weaknesses of the book, they will also make comments about the likely market. Experienced reviewers often have almost as good an understanding of the academic book market in their discipline as publishers. Even if reviewers recommend that the book should be published, they will usually make suggestions about how it might be improved.

If the commissioning editor thinks that the book merits publication in principle, he or she will then write to the author with copies of (or extracts from) the reviewers' reports. He or she will ask for a response to the reviewers' comments, usually indicating those that he/she is particularly concerned about. Reflect carefully about your response. You have to balance the concerns of the publisher and your own wish to defend the integrity of the book. Very often the comments made will be helpful and will lead to a better book, although commercial considerations will necessarily intrude. For example, the publisher might ask (this is a real example) if some references to Australia can be inserted into the book to make it more attractive to the Australian market. On these and more academic issues, there is usually some room for bargaining and compromise. If, however, the publisher wants to fundamentally change the character or emphasis of the book, the author might consider that this would be such a misleading distortion that it would be better to seek another publisher.

If the publisher is prepared to offer a contract, it is useful to clarify what arrangements will be made to sell the book in the important US market. Most publishers have a US 'distributor', but this can amount to little more than taking a limited number of copies and selling the book to libraries who ask for it, and perhaps putting it in an obscure corner of the exhibition stand at major conferences. It is a good idea to ask questions about how the book will be marketed in the United States. Will it be placed in US catalogues, and will there be a separate leaflet attuned to the US market? What presence does the distributor have at major US conferences? If the publisher is not represented through its own offices and operation in the United States (as the major university presses are), the best arrangement may be a US co-publisher who will actively promote the book. If, however, the US market is really important to you, then you should consider having a US publisher in the first place.

No one should expect to make very much or any money out of an academic monograph. The real financial return will come from the contribution the book makes to your efforts to secure a permanent post, or one at a better university, and ultimately promotion to senior lecturer. If your priority is to maximize your short-run financial returns, you should write a textbook or undertake some consultancy (although that latter option is more available in some disciplines than in others). There is, however, a real satisfaction to be derived from receiving the first copy of your first book and turning it over in your hands.

This does not mean that you should not read the contract carefully before you sign it. If royalties are paid at all (sometimes they are paid only after a certain number of copies have been sold), they are usually paid on a 'net receipts' basis, that is, a percentage of the returns received by a publisher after the deduction of discounts to booksellers or other distributors. Academic monographs are usually brought out as hardbacks initially, with a paperback edition perhaps following later, and it as well to check the terms and conditions relating to paperback copies. It is also important to check arrangements relating to electronic publication, which is becoming more important. If you have any concerns, raise them with the publisher. Finally, it is important to agree a realistic submission date with the publisher. Strictly speaking, the contract becomes void if you do not submit the manuscript in a satisfactory form by the agreed date. Publishers rarely withdraw a book offer for this reason, but long delays may make them less willing to deal with you in the future. Remember also that catalogue compilation dates are important deadlines for publishers. Publishers understand-ably dislike authors who assure them that a book is almost complete, because they may then find that they have to explain that a book in their catalogue has in fact not been published.

Turning your PhD into a book

One of the decisions that young academics have to make early in their career is whether to turn their PhD into a book or a number of articles, or indeed not to publish it all. In part this is a disciplinary issue, as in a discipline like economics, whether the PhD provides the basis for, say, two good articles in well-regarded journals is a principal criterion by which it is judged in the first place. In part, it also depends on the contents and structure of the PhD. In most cases, however, you do face an 'either or' choice between a book and articles. This is partly because of time constraints and the need to develop your profile by moving on to your next project. In addition, publishers are likely to be less inter-ested in your proposal if the most innovative and interesting parts of it have already been published as journal articles.

Publishers are understandably wary of proposals to turn PhDs into books. Indeed, sometimes they even give reviewers a set of additional questions to answer about them.

The PhD has a certain format in which students have to meet a number of requirements to show that they have mastered a particular set of skills. The focus of a PhD is often relatively narrow. It often contains a considerable amount of literature review and theoretical discussion that covers relatively familiar ground. The examiner needs to be convinced that the candidate has a full understanding of the intellectual context of his or her study, but readers of a book do not need to be given a tour of territory with which they are probably rela-tively familiar. Indeed, in any book there is a tension between how much knowledge you can assume on the part of readers and the need to explain your own approach sufficiently. You also need to develop a lucid writing style, while recognizing that complexity is part of academic discourse. However, the presentation of complexity should not be done in such a way that it confuses, befuddles or bores the reader.

The originality of the PhD is to be found in the central chapters that probably do not yield enough material for a book. As Lucy commented, 'It's easy if you want to publish it with quite a bad press ...It's very diffi-cult to get it published with a good press unless you're prepared to revise it quite heavily.' Thus even if you do get a contract for a book based on your PhD, you may find reworking it for publication something of a chore, as Zoe did:

> Not terribly easy. It did take me a year to modify it and cut it down from a thesis into a book. It wasn't actually a very fun experience, it's just revisiting stuff you've already done, it's not terribly interesting. In that situation you know you're just doing it for a publication, it's not like doing something new and exciting.

There is an argument for not dwelling too long on your thesis and moving on to new intellectual pastures. As Lucy commented, 'My PhD which I did not want to make into my first big monograph because I just felt that I didn't have the same kind of grasp of what I was doing as I do now.' There is an alternative option, which is to set your thesis aside for a while, apart perhaps from one or two articles, and then return to it and undertake some additional research, which expands its field. This overcomes the objection often made by publishers about narrowness of focus. In most cases, however, the optimum strategy is probably to publish some articles from your PhD in refereed journals and move on to a new and more stimulating challenge.

Edited books

An opportunity may present itself to edit or co-edit a book. Such an opportunity needs to be evaluated very carefully. First, publishers are not very enthusiastic about publishing multi-contributed books because they sell less well than single authored or co-authored books. Prospective purchasers may perceive that they are likely to be of an uneven standard, leading them to photocopy any chapter they are particularly interested in from a library copy rather than buy the book. Any financial return to the editors is likely to be minimal compared with the amount of work involved. Second, a considerable amount of work is usually involved if the edited book is to be more than a compilation of papers presented at a particular event. Contributors need to be encouraged to rewrite their papers to address central themes, although they may be reluctant to do so. The editor needs to write a thematic introduction and probably a conclusion. The whole process may be very frustrating as such books are often held up by one late contribution, which cannot be dropped because it is essential to the completeness of the book. Meanwhile, contributors who delivered on time are complaining because their chapter has become dated. Third,

editing a book has counted for very little in the RAE. This is unfortunate because, if it is done well, it is a skilled and exacting task that can
make a considerable contribution to the development of a particular
theme or debate. The opportunity cost of editing a book can be considerable, so you need to think very carefully before you accept such an
undertaking in the earlier stages of your career.

▶ Refereed journal and other articles

Anyone who wishes to make progress in an academic career outside
a teaching-only institution will have to publish refereed journal articles. In most disciplines, there is now an approximate ranking of the
status of various refereed journals. In some cases there are explicit
lists, although these are always the subject of some controversy. In
many disciplines, the most highly rated journals are those published
by disciplinary associations, with journals published in the United
States ranked more highly than those from the UK or elsewhere in
Europe. However, more specialized journals may also have a high
reputation, and may be good publishing outlets if you are trying to
establish yourself in a particular area of the discipline.

It is, of course, always possible to make an initial submission to a
highly ranked journal and then, if it is rejected, to use the comments
received to improve it for a less highly regarded journal. However, such
a process takes time. It also may mean that you never succeed in
producing a paper that meets the particular requirements of any journal. If the article is relatively specialized, it might go back to the same
referee, who might not be pleased to see it again. As Lauren advised,
'Submitting an article has to be seen as the middle step in a process
rather than the end step. When writing the article have in mind the
journal you are trying to write for.' In a similar vein, Lucy recommended, 'I think that reading as many journal articles as possible helps
you to work out how people are marketing certain essays to certain
types of journals and that can be helpful.'

Many articles start out as conference papers, and the feedback you
receive at the conference can be helpful. Do not feel, however, that you
have to respond to every criticism that has been made. Some commen-
tators will be grinding some axe of their own that has little or no relevance to your own particular concerns. One of the best put-downs
heard at a conference in response to a persistent critic on a particular
point was 'Sure, I'll put in a footnote about that.' Other people may

simply be saying that they do not share your theoretical perspective. The response needed is not to abandon your perspective, but to make sure that you understand it fully, can explain it clearly and defend it against some common criticisms. It is important that you retain your own voice because a journal is not likely to be interested in an article that simply restates prevalent conventional wisdom.

In general, submitting to a journal outside your own discipline carries with it particular hazards, not just in terms of readily under-standing the particular expectations and requirements, such as how evidence is presented and how arguments are made, but also how well the article will be regarded in RAE terms. Area studies journals that cover a number of disciplines may sometimes not be as well regarded as more specialist journals, but may be an appropriate destination for a more interdisciplinary piece. There are, however, some highly regarded journals that exist on the boundaries of disciplines within the humanities and social sciences: for example, politics and history, philosophy and literary studies, sociology and geography, and so on.

It is important to study the requirements of the journal to which you are submitting, not just technical specifications (Harvard system of referencing versus footnotes, mode of submission, and so on) but in particular the length of article that is expected. Some journals will, of course, accept research notes or comments as well as articles, and these may be a particularly appropriate form of publication for a new entrant. However, they will not substitute on your CV for full-length academic journal articles. If your article is excessively long, it is more likely to be rejected out of hand as the editor will not want to trouble busy referees with it. If the article is too short, the editor may suggest its resubmission as a note, which is perhaps what it should have been in the first place. If the journal uses abstracts, as almost all reputable ones do, it is worth spending some time on crafting this as it allows you to make a succinct statement of the distinctiveness and value added offered by the article. Make sure that your article is free of gram-matical and spelling errors and typos, is properly laid out and pagi-nated, and that all works cited are fully referenced. Referees tend to look unfavourably on articles that show signs of having been completed in a hurry, reflected in sloppy presentation.

Five recurrent faults
Experience of reviewing hundreds of articles for refereed journals suggests five recurrent faults, some of which may be particularly displayed by less experienced authors. First, authors take too long to

get to the point, by which is meant what they have to say that is new and distinctive, whether it is terms of theory, methodology or empirical findings. There is often too much review of existing literature, something to which new entrants may be particularly prone, given their recent experience of writing a PhD. Admittedly, this is encouraged by some journals and their referees, particularly US journals, who expect every relevant reference to be cited. It is certainly not a good idea to omit any mention of established authorities, as they may serve as referees. However, pressured referees are likely to be exasperated by a long survey of familiar territory.

Second, and again this is a fault that less experienced writers may be particularly prone to, there is a tendency to be either excessively deferential to existing authorities in the field, or dismissive or scathing. If you follow the first course of action, you may fail to make key points that help you to establish your argument. However, if you dismiss their position as 'dated' or 'no longer credible', a referee who is a member of the school that has been attacked will immediately leap to its defence. At best, you may then find yourself asked to produce a long elaboration of your position which actually detracts from your central argument.

Third, while using terminology appropriate to and accepted in your discipline, clarity in what you write is important. There sometime seems to be an assumption that a somewhat elliptical writing style is itself evidence of academic seriousness. It is interesting to contrast practice in the natural sciences with the humanities and social sciences in this respect. As part of a joint research project with natural scientists, colleagues in biological sciences were asked to read some well-regarded articles in social science journals. They were surprised at how digressive and discursive they were in contrast to the much tauter writing style deployed in the natural sciences. Sometimes as a referee one gets the sense that one is in a circular journey where the central point is always just as far away but is never reached.

Fourth, the conclusion is often the most disappointing part of the article, instead of lifting it to a final crescendo. Good conclusions are not easy to write, particularly concluding sentences. One often senses that authors have become exhausted, or have run out of time and space when they have reached this point, throwing together some concluding remarks as an afterthought. Considerable care should be taken with the conclusion. It should bring together the key points made in the article, demonstrating their significance and suggesting what the implications for future research might be.

Fifth, the extent to which substantive footnotes are allowed or encouraged will vary from journal to journal and discipline to discipline. However, even where their use is seen as a means of demonstrating the depth of your scholarship, try to be sparing in their deployment. The reader constantly has to be looking to the bottom of the page or the end of the article, interrupting the flow of reading the article. It is then disconcerting to often find that the substantive footnotes contain arguments or evidence that are of central importance. A good test to apply to any substantive footnote is to ask whether it is so significant that it should be included in the text, or so insignificant that it can be left out without detracting from the argument being made.

When the editor or member of an editorial team receives an article, the first decision that is usually made is whether the article is to be sent out to referees at all. The article might be not of the right length, insufficiently related to the journal's mission or not academic enough in its content. Sometimes a member of the editorial board might be consulted before such a decision is made. In any event, you will be informed relatively quickly of the outcome. Such a rapid rejection does not mean that the article is of an insufficiently high standard, it simply means you have sent it to the wrong journal.

One of the frustrating aspects of submitting a journal article is the time it takes before you receive a decision. Articles are sent out to two or three referees who might have several articles a month to review. It is a task that requires careful attention and one that should not be hurried. The editor will have to wait for the last referee's report to be submitted. The editor might then face contradictory reports that require further reflection on the editor's part and possibly further consultation.

Outright rejection can be a heavy blow, particularly early in a career. It is important not to be too disheartened. As Luke recalled:

> Don't be too disheartened if people turn you down. I've only ever had one outright rejection and it felt like a body blow, it really did. Refereeing is not a perfect science.

It is important not to take rejection as a sign that you are following the wrong strategy. As Lucy commented:

> The first article I sent out was quite seriously criticized. In the end a lot of people are paralysed by the idea that it's not perfect and they shouldn't send it out and I have sent a lot of stuff out and I think got a lot of stuff accepted and rejected.

Do not seek to challenge the decision that has been taken by the editors, even when the editor has overruled favourable reports recommending publication. They are very unlikely to change it. Complaining that the decision was ill-founded or unfair will damage your reputation with leading members of the discipline, and in any case editors are usually unwilling to engage in a correspondence with authors who are dissatisfied with their decision.

The process of producing a refereed journal article can be long-drawn-out, but persistence can bring its rewards both in terms of eventual publication and a better article. As Amy recalled:

> We originally thought [a conference paper] was going to get into the proceedings; six months later they told us that wasn't going ahead after we'd written it up for that, so then we had to change the whole emphasis of it and took it to [a journal]. We thought it had a good chance, then eventually after about eight months it was rejected, so then we found another journal, we changed the whole focus again and also had to change the references. It was accepted there. It's a much better paper for all of that, so it was about a three-year process and really changing the direction.

Your article is unlikely to be accepted outright. Most articles that are eventually published have to go through a process of revision and resubmission. Practices between journals vary, but often editors instruct referees not to recommend revision and submission unless there is a real chance that the work can be published, to avoid unnecessary work and disappointment. Some journals ask referees to indicate on response forms how serious the revision required is. The process of resubmission is not an easy one for the author as Zoe noted:

> When things get accepted with changes you just have to grit your teeth and accept the changes even though sometimes it's hard because you wrote the article in a certain way because you thought that was the way it should be done and if you want to get it published, sometimes you have to get on with making the changes they want. It's always horrible having to modify something you think you've already finished.

This does not mean that there is no room for negotiation. Indeed, quite often, the reports from referees are contradictory and editors will often indicate which changes they regard as not essential and which they will insist on before publication. Some of the most difficult criticisms to deal with are those relating to omissions rather than to things you have actually said, as they require substantial additions to the article, which means that you then have to remove material elsewhere and the whole structure can fall apart. There is then a risk that the resubmitted article is actually worse than the original version. If you do receive a revise and resubmit decision, take your time over your response despite the temptation to get the matter resolved one way or another. Even if you are able to make the requested changes relatively quickly, too quick a resubmission may suggest that you have been insufficiently thorough and unduly hasty. If you find some of the required changes difficult to make or troubling to your intellectual integrity, you need to consider what to do carefully, taking advice from your peers and more senior colleagues (although the latter are likely to be predisposed to securing publication at almost any price). Ultimately, if you cannot reach a mutually acceptable agreement with the editor, you have to defend the integrity of your message and not proceed with publication in that journal, even if that is not easy in the context of RAE pressures.

Occasionally an article will receive a reply, to which you will usually be entitled to publish a rejoinder. Editors usually like to encourage debate based on articles that they have published. Do not be concerned about the fact that your article has attracted a reply. It is a sign that your article has made an impact and is considered worth responding to. If the reply article has some strong points that lead you to modify the position, be prepared to consider them. There is nothing wrong with displaying intellectual flexibility. Equally, be willing to rebut any misunderstandings or misrepresentations of your position. Given that your response will be limited in length, try to focus on key points of the argument rather than matters of detail. A debate of this kind will attract wider attention to your work and you might come to be seen as being representative of a particular position.

Web-based journals are becoming increasingly common. By this is meant journals that are published only in electronic form, as distinct from the increasing availability of journals and articles electronically. Such journals are not generally as well regarded as those journals that also appear in print form, although in part this may because electronic journals have been established more recently. One of their advantages is that they can generally publish articles much more quickly, so they may be an appropriate form of publication if you have an article that is particularly topical. They may also be associated with new and emerging schools of thought, and building your reputation with such a group that represents a wave of the future might pay off in the long run. It is important that you find out whether articles in the particular journal are subject to a peer review process that is as rigorous as that which applies in most print journals. It would not be wise to publish just in web-based journals, although their reputation is likely to rise over time. For some articles, they may be the most suitable outlet.

In some cases it may be appropriate to publish in journals that are not refereed but are read extensively, particularly by practitioners. This may be particularly relevant in disciplines like law and social policy where there is a clear relationship between the academic discipline and a defined group of practitioners. There may be differences within disciplines in this respect. Within political science, public policy specialists may be eager to address politicians through journals that range from the quasi-academic to house journals for the political class, while a mediaeval political theorist would have less interest in and opportunity to address such an audience. Many disciplines have publications aimed at 16–18 year olds working towards university. Such articles often attract a fee and are worth doing if you can write them relatively quickly on a subject with which you are familiar. There may also be opportunities to write for newspapers and popular magazines. This may have the added attraction of a fee. However, the same objections apply as to broadcast media work. Too much writing of this kind may attract the envious attention of colleagues who will question your seriousness. An article on Jane Austen in a colour supplement will not receive the same approbation as one published in a well-regarded academic journal.

▶ Other forms of publication

The book chapter is sometimes unfairly derided as a form of publication in the context of the RAE, but leading academics in major research universities are still willing to write book chapters. One of its advantages is that you have a relatively high assurance of publication, as it is relatively unusual for an invited book chapter to then be rejected outright by the editor. A difficult dilemma you may face is if you are asked by a senior figure to turn a conference paper into a book chapter. One consideration to bear in mind is how far the editor is likely to want you to change what you have written to fit in with the theme of the book. This raises questions both of workload and of how far the points you want to make are going to be diluted. On the other hand, it may present an opportunity to write both a book chapter and a refereed journal article out of the paper. However, a CV that is over-weighted towards book chapters compared with refereed journal articles will not help you when it comes to applying for jobs. It is also worth bearing in mind that edited books can take a long time to produce, which is of particular significance if your material is likely to date.

Book reviews are a means of getting your name known and also of getting hold of copies of books that you might not otherwise afford. Many journals are keen to encourage younger academics as reviewers, and it is possible to provide them with details of your interests. Book reviews vary in length from the book note of 200 words (or even less), in which it is difficult to do more than outline the main features of the book and make a brief comment on its worth, to longer reviews of 800 or 1000 words, which offer the opportunity to provide a more sustained critique of a book and place it within a broader context. If you are offered the opportunity to write a review article looking at a number of related books, this is even more worthwhile. It will be a longer piece, perhaps as much as 2000 or 3000 words, will have a higher profile and attract much more attention than a book note. However, such an invited article is not a substitute for a refereed journal article, particularly in terms of the RAE. If you have written a lot of book reviews, do not pad your CV out with them as they are unlikely to be given a very high weighting. It is more impressive to list the journals for which you have reviewed if they are highly regarded.

Sometimes you may be asked to write encyclopaedia entries, either for general encyclopaedias or for discipline specific publications, which may be called 'dictionaries'.

General encyclopaedias usually have very specific guidelines about how entries should be written and it might be quite difficult to adjust your style to their requirements. Accuracy is also of central importance. Discipline-specific dictionaries often require short entries of perhaps 100 words, and this is a particular skill. If you are a person who is capable of writing tautly and adjusting your style to particular requirements, the fees paid may make this kind of work worth it. However, do not do too much of it as you will get little academic credit for your efforts. As with all secondary forms of publication, it is always advisable to take account of the opportunity costs in terms of work not done on research monographs or refereed journal articles. Above all, do not be tempted by an offer to get involved in editing an encyclopaedia. Because of the number of authors involved, the coordination costs are very high, and can eat into your time and be a considerable source of frustration.

Websites are an increasingly important means of getting your work across to a variety of audiences. Publishers increasingly ask for them to accompany books, and research councils may insist on them as a condition of research grants. If your department allocates you a web page, make sure it provides a concise account of your interests. If possible, have samples of published work available for downloading. You need to be cautious about making work that you have not finished accessible on a website. Websites can be a useful means of bringing the contemporary relevance of your work to the attention of people outside the academic profession, including decision makers and the media. They provide an opportunity to write about your work in a lighter, more informal style. If you are interested in consultancy work, websites may make your interests and expertise known to potential clients.

► Co-authorship

During the course of your career many opportunities will present themselves for co-authorship in relation to all forms of publication. One golden rule to bear in mind is to avoid a CV in which almost everything is co-authored, which is more common than might be supposed. Such a CV may suggest to prospective employers that you do not have a distinctive voice of your own and that much of your work has taken the form of the provision of research materials to others who then write them up, even if this is not the case. However, the absence of any co-authored work may suggest that you are not very good at working collaboratively with others.

Bearing that important qualification in mind, co-authorship presents the opportunity to produce work that is more than the sum of its parts. It works best when you work with someone who offers complementary skills to yours. For example, it could be someone from another discipline; someone who can bring a body of theoretical work to the analysis with which you are not familiar; someone from another country who can contribute to a comparative study; or someone who has a body of empirical material that complements your own. What is important is to agree a clear division of labour between you and an approximate timetable for completion of the work.

Electronic communication has greatly reduced the costs of co-authorship, particularly between countries, but there is no substitute for meeting together to discuss the work face to face. This is particularly important in the case of a co-authored book. It is important to avoid a disjuncture in style and approach between the different chapters.

Someone has to produce drafts of chapters or parts of them. However, the best co-authored books are often produced when the authors have worked intensively together on the manuscript. The rewards can then be considerable. As Lucy commented:

> As soon as you've got strong friends within your field, that's when the best work starts to emerge. I'm writing a book with somebody at the moment, it's just been a great experience and that's just somebody I met at a conference.

Serendipity can play a key role in the emergence of co-authors. Some of the contacts will be relatively casual and will be limited to one publication. Others may lead to collaborations that will endure over an academic lifetime. How can you select a suitable co-author? In particular, what are the relative advantages and disadvantages of working with someone who is a senior, established person compared with someone who is a peer?

The senior person may have more contacts that facilitate publication, but you may find yourself doing most of the work for a publication for which the other person takes half the credit. Indeed, because of their standing senior people may be perceived as the main contributors. Of course, the opposite can happen: senior academics can find their names exploited by new entrants who then expect them to do most of the work. You may feel more comfortable working with a peer, particularly if you share a new perspective or area of study that is emerging in your discipline.

This is really an area in which you have to exercise personal judgement. It should be possible to work very well with a more senior person who is on the same intellectual wavelength on you, is a secure and well-integrated person and treats you as an intellectual equal. Many senior academics have a genuine wish to repay the help they were given at an early stage of their career. Equally, you need to avoid senior academics who are insecure personalities, over-preoccupied with their own status and ready to exploit the understanding of new perspectives possessed by younger colleagues. Often their reputation precedes them, but it is possible to be flattered by the attention of a more senior colleague.

With your peers it is important to try to establish that they are reliable and have good work habits. This does not mean whether they have a tidy office or not, as it is possible for apparent chaos to conceal underlying organization. What is more relevant is whether they are inclined to take too much work on, and whether they can schedule that work properly. It is also necessary to consider whether they have strong and rigid views on particular matters, which might make co-authorship difficult. It is not necessary to be particularly friendly with a co-author, as the relationship is essentially a professional one, but friendship may grow out of the professional collaboration.

Whether you should co-author with a partner is a decision that only you can make. Work could be disrupted by strains in the personal relationship, and it could introduce new strains into that relationship. Equally, the shared project could have a strengthening effect. Some relationships flourish on the basis of spending work and leisure time together, but many people like to have a measure of autonomy even in a close relationship, and a space they call their own, most often a working space.

▶ The mechanics of publication

The mechanics of publication for a book chapter or refereed journal article are relatively straightforward. In the case of a book chapter, checking of the proofs is often done by the editor of the book. You have to check the proofs for refereed journal articles, but this is to correct errors made by the printer, not to make changes in substance or style. This section therefore concentrates on the publication of a book.

Once your manuscript has been submitted to the publisher and approved for publication, it will be sent to a copy editor, to mark it up for the printer and also to present you with a list of queries relating to questions of both style and substance. Dealing with these queries can be quite a time-consuming part of the book production process. They need to be handled quickly, as otherwise the production of the book will be delayed. The culture of copy editing seems to be different in the United States from that in the UK, with copy editors in North America taking a more activist stance towards the manuscript. Indeed, it is not unknown for reviews in the *New York Times Book Review* to complain that copy editors have not been interventionist enough!

Luey (2002, p. 96) offers good advice on how to relate to copy editors:

1. This is your book, and the ideas and general style should remain yours.
2. The editor is not an expert in your field, but that editor is an expert in scholarly publishing, and you should listen to advice of that sort offered.

3. Editorial changes should not be taken as personal insults.
4. You and the editor are on the same side, and both of you want the book to be as good as possible.

When you receive the proofs of the book you will not only have to read them carefully for errors, you will also have to prepare an index. One way of thinking about an index is as a detailed list of contents. This is an important part of producing a high-quality book, as it will be consulted extensively by individuals who do not have time to read the book as a whole, but want to see what it has to say on particular topics. It is a time-consuming task that has to be undertaken against tight deadlines. You could, of course, hire a professional indexer, although it is important to ensure that you use someone who is familiar with academic as distinct from more general books. The cost of hiring such a person is likely to exceed the royalties you earn from the book. You could hire a graduate student, perhaps using departmental funds, but he or she is not likely to do a particularly good job.

The best indexes are often prepared by authors who really understand the structure of their manuscript, but they have to bear in mind that the index is a tool for readers to enable them to make the best use of the book. Sometimes there are two separate indexes, with one for the names of persons and proper names, and the other for general entries. Indeed, this may be a matter of the publisher's house style, but combined indexes are generally more helpful to the reader and easier to compile.

Some publishers provide their authors with a guide to preparing an index, but the following hints may be useful:

- Remember to include the name of everyone you have cited in the text. Academics can be quite vain and will turn to the index to see if they have been cited.
- Make sure that you spell names correctly, and do not confuse authors with the same name.
- Ensure that your key theories and concepts are fully indexed.
- Make sure that you include sufficient cross-references to where similar matters are discussed, of the kind 'see also postmodernism'.
- Make sufficient use of sub-entries for your key concepts.
- If your book has a chronological and biographical element relating to a particular person, make sure that you have a comprehensive time line of entries relating to particular stages of the person's

career, for example, Austen, Jane: birth, 2; final illness and move to Winchester, 207–23; friendship with Martha Lloyd, 37–41; move to Bath, 27–33, 46; move to Chawton, 118–21, and so on.

When your book appears, it is worth registering it for public lending right. You should already have taken up membership of the Authors' Licensing and Copyright Society (ALCS) if you have published book chapters or refereed journal articles, but if you have not already done this, you should do so. (See Box 6.2.)

When reviews of your book appear, some of them will be critical. Occasionally, you may think that your book has been unfairly treated. 'It rarely does any good to object to a review' (Luey, 2002, p. 104). In the unlikely event of the journal publishing your response, it will only

---

Box 6.2   Maximizing revenue from your published work

Public lending right

Public lending right (PLR) payments are based on borrowings from a sample of public libraries in the UK. No payment is made if the sum accrued is under £5. Payments are more likely on textbooks or on books in the humanities, which have some popular appeal.

Payments tend to be higher in the early years after publication. You should not expect a large amount, but registration is free online at http://www.plr.uk.com

Copyright payments

The Authors' Licensing and Copyright Society (ALCS) collects and distributes fees to writers whose works have been copied, broadcast or recorded. Photocopying is the largest source of income and the fees are collected by the Copyright Licensing Agency on the basis of a random sampling procedure. Payments made include sums for photocopying overseas (not attributed to specific titles) and from the equivalents of PLR schemes in other countries such as Germany and Sweden. The sums received can be quite considerable. ALCS funds its activities by deducting a commission from payments, which is reduced for its members. Full information is available at http://www.alcs.co.uk

draw more attention to the unfavourable review. It will also give the impression that you are a person who does not know how to accept and deal with criticism. It is also unwise to enter into an acrimonious correspondence with the reviewer. Try to learn what you can from reviews for your future work, but accept that there will be the occasional review that simply fails to understand what you have been trying to achieve in your book.

▶ Conclusions

The impact of electronic publication

Journal publication has already been transformed by electronic forms of publication. Most academic journals are now sold in packages, which enable a library or group of libraries to have not just a print copy, but also to allow their members to access copies of articles online. There are some journals that publish just in an electronic format, and they are generally able to publish articles more quickly, but they are often less well regarded than more established journals. The cost of purchasing journals for libraries has been rising much faster than the rate of inflation, and this has led to calls for entirely new modes of publication. It is possible that the traditional subscription model could eventually be replaced by a system whereby authors pay to have papers published and the content is then freely available on the Internet. This might seem like a new form of vanity publishing, but the fees could be covered by universities, who would save money on journal subscriptions, or out of research grants. The fees could, however, be substantial. The House of Commons Science and Technology Committee has already recommended that universities should be required to ensure that all their research papers are available free online, and that government-funded research grants ought to make free access to research findings a condition of the awards. Any change in forms of publishing would have to preserve the integrity of the peer review process to satisfy RAE pressures.

As far as books are concerned, 'We are in the middle of the biggest revolution in the world of content creation and publication since Caxton invented the printing press' (Charkin, 2005, p. 2). It is increasingly possible to purchase an electronic copy of a book, although most sales are still made in the traditional format. Sample chapters are placed on publishers' websites to entice readers to buy the book. Quite how the digital revolution will develop remains to be seen; in part it is dependent on the legal and other debates surrounding Google's plans to digitize books and make them available online. Some of the questions that arise include: are 'online' and 'offline' separate market places? Will 'print on demand' and 'never out of print' be factors in future publishing markets? Will the book publishing industry follow the music industry into an illicit file transfer and download culture (www.googledebate.com)? Wider use of digital technologies may benefit consumers, but will they further erode the position of authors?

Metrics and the future of the RAE

The Office of Science and Technology's (OST) public service agreement target requires it to show the health of the UK research base, including the international standing of research in the UK. The OST decided that citations data should be the measure of quality for the UK research base, although 'The Web of Knowledge's coverage is heavily biased towards the United States and towards English-language journals more generally' (Dunleavy, 2003, p. 230). Government, however, tends to have a preference for quantitative data, even if it is imperfect. The Arts and Humanities Research Council successfully argued that a citations-based approach could not be used for the arts and humanities, and was required to produce an alternative. It developed the idea of a journal reference list that would enable a calculation of the proportion of articles in journals of international standing that were from the UK. The actual development of this list is likely to be a difficult task, but once available, it will certainly have an influence on what are seen as the top journals in the humanities.

In general, the use of metrics tends to privilege journals over other forms of publishing, pushing the humanities and social sciences more towards a natural science model. Yet 'the median journal article is referred to by nobody in the five years after it is published, and very few articles have a referencing life longer than this' (Dunleavy, 2003, p. 230). Respect for the research monograph remains strong in the humanities and in many of the social sciences.

Academics cannot ignore RAE requirements because their universities and departments will pressurize them to conform to them. Consultants from other universities are increasingly being hired to check internal evaluations. How can these pressures be balanced with your desire to develop your own voice and contribute to the development of scholarship? Not easily, but once you have fulfilled your RAE requirements, you then have more freedom to publish what you want.

The 2008 RAE is likely to be the last one, given that it has now largely achieved its implicit objective of producing a stratification of institutions and departments in the UK in terms of levels of research activity. It could be replaced by some form of continuous benchmarking, which could increase the extent to which forms of publication are shaped by external considerations. This would imply that departments would be subject to periodic reviews to see whether their rankings were still justified. There could also be a further move away from dual funding of research whereby money is provided both by HEFCE and its equivalents and by the research councils. Indeed, full economic costing already represents a shift towards providing funding through the research councils, which some influential voices advocate. While this may in principle seem to be a more democratic way of providing funding open to all competitors, in practice it would not operate like that. It would also increase the pressures on the individual researcher who, at least in principle and in some departments, has access to a stream of 'R' funding from HEFCE. These issues are discussed further in the next chapter.

7 Obtaining and Managing Research Grants

Most of the young academics we talked to in the course of writing this book had little or no experience of applying for research grants, certainly on their own. Emma remarked, 'I find the thought of research grants quite horrific in terms of what they're looking for.' A record of successfully obtaining research grants is, however, increasingly becoming a criterion for promotion.

▶ Full economic costing

The shift to full economic costing (FEC) from September 2005 also increases the pressure on academics to obtain research grants. This could eventually mean the end of the dual support system of research funding where money for research is provided from HEFCE in relation to RAE outcomes and through the research councils. This could provide additional opportunities for post-1992 universities that have difficulty in doing well in the RAE to obtain funding, although it also increases the transaction costs involved in obtaining research funding.

FEC would in principle recover the total cost (direct, indirect and total overhead) spent by a university on research, including an adequate recurring investment in the institution's infrastructure. It should therefore overcome cross-subsidization, for example through the principal investigator's salary. In the past, universities have been unsure of the real costs of research, including research equipment, library costs and staff time. It is estimated that research grants have covered only about half of these costs.

One problem with FEC is that different research sponsors may be prepared to pay different proportions of identified costs. Universities will tend to favour those sponsors that will pay the largest proportion of costs, whereas researchers may find a research sponsor who is less generous more attractive for other reasons. Research councils will pay a price that is set at a percentage of 80 per cent of FEC. Other government sponsors should usually pay a price set at 100 per cent of FEC. However, charitable foundations and the EU are likely to continue to maintain their own set of rules about cost estimates and the price paid will depend on those rules. Charities are likely to pay much less than 100 per cent of FEC.

FEC will cover five components of cost. Academic and researcher staff time and costs will include additional research staff employed for the project and an estimate of the time spent by the principal investigator or co-investigators on project management. Technical and clerical staff costs may also be charged to the project. Direct non-staff costs include not only costs directly incurred for the project, but also the cost of services shared with other projects or activities, for example, library and information technology costs. Estate costs can also be directly allocated to research projects, although these will necessarily be higher for laboratory-based projects. Finally, it will be possible to charge other indirect costs to the project. The rules covering the operation of these arrangements, and the monitoring and auditing methods used, will necessarily be complex, and academics will need to rely on advice from their university research service organizations.

▶ First steps towards a research grant

Four general pieces of advice are worth bearing in mind. First, normally your first attempt at obtaining a research grant should be made with others, preferably including an experienced senior researcher. In this way, you will learn about the procedures and techniques involved in obtaining a grant. As Ruth commented, 'I suppose the main thing is that there is a formula, a knack or technique in telling the funder what it is you want to do in a way that will give you the money.' There may be occasions when you want to apply for a grant for a very specific purpose such as visiting an archive and then an application on your own is quite appropriate. As Luke pointed out being a stand-alone single researcher 'gives you control of the project, but it also puts you under a lot of pressure'.

Second, make full use of your university's research services section. As Luke commented, 'they may be a resource that is under-used'. Its staff will have experience of dealing with research sponsors on a regular basis, and will know what they are looking for in terms of themes, and what their particular requirements are in terms of information in the application. Many university research services section run training events for young researchers and these are usually worth attending. If your university does not have research support services, or they are inadequately resourced, perhaps you are in the wrong university if you want to pursue research.

Third, when you make your first research grant application on your own, consider smaller-scale research grants, details of which are given later in the chapter. Zoe successfully obtained a small research grant. She recalled,

> It's very, very targeted, it's not one of the big grant-making bodies, I knew at the time I was very much tapping into one of their key areas so I think that's why it was successful as opposed to going for something bigger with a much bigger organization which may have been less likely to be successful.

Smaller grants usually involve less onerous form filling, you get a decision more quickly and there are less arduous reporting requirements.

Fourth, make sure that you have sufficient time to complete the research grant application and then to undertake the research. Do not underestimate the amount of time that is required for the preparation of a good research application. A proposal that is put together in a hurry is unlikely to meet quality standards. Many grant applications have to be submitted in accordance with very tight deadlines and involve complex forms, not least those of the EU. This means that you need to be prepared well in advance by having familiarized yourself with the priorities of the particular research sponsor. It is also useful to familiarize yourself with the technical details of an application by reading through the relevant rules and regulations. Incomplete applications or those that do not provide the required information are likely to be discarded. It is helpful to have well-regarded referees, so make sure that they are lined up in advance and expect to be asked for a reference.

It is perhaps understandable if applicants focus on getting the grant rather than on what they are going to do when it has been awarded. Having obtained the grant, don't place oneself in the position of Zoe, who admitted, 'The snag is I haven't had the time to spend it.'

Preparing a proposal
Box 7.1 sets up some useful general principles for preparing a proposal for funding. One useful general principle to bear in mind is parsimony:

Box 7.1 Preparing your research proposal

These informal guidelines were provided by the Economic and Social Research Council (ESRC), but they have a wider applicability.

Your research plan:

- Set your basic funding argument down on paper first. Frame the problem you will be addressing, provide the context and explain what your contribution will be.
- Prove to the assessor that you are the person to undertake this research – underline the skills and abilities necessary for success.
- Ensure that your requirements (in terms of scale, timings and resources) are reasonably argued.
- Demonstrate that you have carefully considered your data collection methodology, including whether to use existing data resources, and how you will access or collect the data, as well as how you will approach the analysis. [In the case of the humanities you will need to indicate, for example, what archives are available or where you will be able to examine the works of art that form part of your study.]
- Set out your financial needs clearly, don't over or under cost, and give a detailed breakdown of your anticipated requirements. Lavish costings are unlikely to find favour, and a proposal that promises the earth at remarkably low cost will be regarded with caution.
- Include dissemination activities in your research plan – the ESRC is placing a new emphasis on user engagement and this shouldn't just be an afterthought.
- Indicate that you have thought through any potential difficulties and outline a contingency plan for handling them.
- Finally, use plain English – your readers won't all be experts in your field. And proofread – unchecked applications look careless and hasty.

---

for example, parsimony in the scope of what you intend to do, the theoretical perspectives you plan to apply and the resources that you expect to consume. Parsimony is also important in terms of describing the project, as you will have a limited number of words at your disposal or a constrained space to answer particular questions on the form.

Given that many sponsors ask for a one-sentence description of the project in plain English, it is often helpful to write this at an early stage to clarify in your own mind what you are trying to achieve. This can be followed by writing the short description of the research. In the application every word will have to count, so avoid flowery sentences or superfluous words. Avoid vague statements such as 'Interviews may be conducted with ...' or 'Further archives will be visited if time allows.'

The general principles advanced by the Economic and Social Research Council (ESRC) reproduced in Box 7.1 will be expanded and commented on in the text, making use of a hypothetical example. A young economist working in a business school is interested in the fact that Iceland, a country with a very small population, has become a source of significant foreign direct investment (FDI), particularly in the United Kingdom.

It is important to demonstrate that you have a research problem that is interesting, important and reasonably novel. There are few topics of any significance that have not been researched at all, so you will need to demonstrate that you are aware of the existing literature and that you can take it a stage further, usually both theoretically and empirically. Of course, some projects may be entirely theoretical in emphasis and others will be predominantly empirical, but most projects have a balance of both elements. In the case of the hypothetical example, the researcher would need to be clear about the primary objective. Is the main interest in why and how Iceland has been able to fund so much FDI, or is the principal concern the impact of the FDI on recipient countries?

In accordance with the second principle, you need to show why you are the person who should undertake the research. The research topic may be a worthwhile one, but are you the best qualified to undertake it? Qualifications would include earlier work in the area of the research and any necessary technical or linguistic skills. In the case of the imaginary economist, he is fortunate enough to have an Icelandic mother so he has relevant linguistic skills. He can also show that he has done earlier work on the Icelandic economy and has a more general interest in FDI.

It is important to have a realistic idea of what you can achieve in a given period of time. Younger researchers often underestimate how time-consuming a particular piece of research is likely to be. It is important to set boundaries around the research that make it feasible without narrowing the focus so much that it ceases to be interesting. This is actually difficult even for experienced researchers. There is a natural tendency to want to cover as much as possible and not leave interesting issues out.

In the hypothetical example, the researcher decides to concentrate on the impact of Icelandic FDI. This allows him to avoid difficult controversies about whether some of the Icelandic FDI may have been funded by money from Russia. Instead he can use the existing literature to see if there is anything distinctive about Icelandic FDI, for example in terms of corporate strategy or employment policies. In order to provide a tighter focus to the research, it is decided to concentrate on sectors of the UK economy where Icelandic investment has been particularly important, for example, retailing.

Data collection methodology is more important for the social sciences. Indeed, one of the areas in which social science applications most frequently fail is methodology. However, methodological considerations are not irrelevant to the humanities, particularly in the broad sense of 'a study of the principles and theories which guide the choice of method' (Burnham, Gilland, Grant and Layton-Henry, 2004, p. 4) rather than the choice of particular research techniques. Humanities sponsors will need to be assured that you will have access to the data you need: for example, relevant documents are available in publicly accessible archives and not subject to closure restrictions, or art collections can be viewed even if they are in storage or in private hands. In the social sciences, much can be achieved through the re-analysis of existing data sets available in archives such as that of the ESRC or through the utilization of official statistics. As May notes (2001, p. 71):

> The amount of material routinely collected by the government and its agencies provides a rich source of data for the social researcher. With CD-ROMs and access to data sets via the internet now available, technology has afforded researchers greater access to information and with that, more opportunities for secondary data analysis.

Collecting your own data in the social sciences can be very expensive, and it is therefore important to ensure that you have exhausted all possibilities of the re-analysis of existing data. In the humanities it is increasingly possible to search archive catalogues online. In our hypothetical example, the researcher decides that much of the information about FDI flows and trends can be extracted from official data in the UK and Iceland, allowing a focus in the research on interviews with Icelandic investors to explore their intentions and strategies.

Financial needs are often an area where research applications fail. Remember that as far as the research sponsor is concerned, the more that is spent on your project, the less that is available for other projects. Research sponsors will often ask referees to comment on the value for money offered by the application: that is, the balance between the costs of the research and its likely benefits. Applicants are often vague about why particular sums of money are required, for example, '£1000 for Xeroxing', which can look like a subsidy for the departmental budget, or an amount for clerical help when there is no clear need for it. Applicants may want to make too many field trips at too great a cost. Equally, it is important to ask for sufficient funds to achieve what you plan to do. This is why it is important to set clear, well-defined boundaries around the project at an early stage.

In the hypothetical example, travel to Iceland and accommodation and other costs there are relatively high, so the researcher seeks to restrict the number of trips to the minimum necessary and to conduct interviews in the UK whenever possible.

ESRC places particular emphasis on dissemination and engagement with 'stakeholders', but most research sponsors will want some idea of the academic and other outputs likely to result from the research. As far as academic outputs are concerned, these must be proportionate to the sum of money asked for. For a small grant of less than £10,000, a research monograph or two articles in well-regarded journals might be regarded as sufficient. However, for a grant of £100,000, the same level of output would clearly be insufficient. You also need to show that you have given some thought to where the material might be placed. Even if you do not mention specific journals, you should specify peer-reviewed journals and give some idea of the mix between outlets in the UK and elsewhere, particularly in North America. While you would not be expected to have a book contract, an indication of interest from specific publishers is helpful. It is important to be as precise as possible about where the work will be disseminated. It is no good saying 'at conferences'; you need to say which ones and why they are relevant.

As far as dissemination of results outside the world of academia is concerned, a website is always a good way of reaching a variety of audiences. If you have taken any courses in website design, mention this, or if you would be able to call on support from your university's information technology service to design the site and get it up and running. Particularly in the social sciences, workshops for practitioners, perhaps organized in conjunction with a think tank in London, are usually a good idea. If your material is suitable for dissemination in the media, mention the kinds of outlets that might be relevant: for example, radio broadcasts, broadsheet papers, weekly magazines or the specialist trade press.

You will also be given credit for giving forethought to any possible problems, for example, 'The archive at Pavia may be closed for building work during the course of the project and this may take longer than the forecast six months. In that event some of the materials are available in archives in Milano and Firenze and the work at Pavia will be rescheduled.' Finally, although it is necessary to demonstrate a familiarity with relevant academic terminology, it is important to show that your skills include an ability to communicate effectively with those who are not expert in the field. This is particularly important when your research has some policy relevance.

Some larger grants may involve a two-stage process in which a preliminary proposal is submitted and then a subset of proposers are invited to enter a final stage. It is disappointing to be knocked out at the first stage, but at least the considerable work in submitting a full application is avoided. Preliminary applications usually require less detail about financial aspects of the project, which can be the most time-consuming to complete. It is, however, important to be particularly clear about the objectives to be pursued and how these relate to the thematic priorities of the potential sponsor.

▶ Selecting a research sponsor

The most important sources of research funding are the research councils, the British Academy, the charitable foundations and (mainly for social scientists) EU and UK government departments. Occasionally a small and relatively obscure charity may be an ideal funding source for a small-scale project, especially in the humanities. The Directory of Social Change publishes a CD-ROM of grant-making trusts in association with the Charities Aid Foundation, which covers 4500 trusts (http://www.dsc.org.uk).

Many of these trusts have no relevance to academic research, however. Most researchers will be seeking to obtain funds from the research councils and the charitable foundations, and these are the main focus of the discussion here. Some universities have their own research funds, and these can be useful for pilot projects or preliminary work. There is often an expectation that the internal funding will lead to an application to an external research sponsor.

In selecting a potential research sponsor, the younger researcher needs to bear the following criteria in mind:

- Does it fund the areas in which you are interested? Both research councils and charitable foundations are placing increasing emphasis on thematic priorities, and this can pose problems for more traditional curiosity-driven research. Can your own research interests be adapted to fit in with a sponsor's priorities?
- Does it have smaller grant schemes that are suitable for a first research application, and does it generally encourage younger researchers?
- Are its forms reasonably straightforward to complete?
- Make sure you are up to date with what is happening at a research sponsor by consulting its website (see Box 7.2). Funding priorities and initiatives may change quite quickly, and occasionally an organization may be radically restructured and its priorities may change or the funds available may be reduced.

Research councils

For most of the readers of this book the two relevant research councils are the Arts and Humanities Research Council (AHRC, formerly the Arts and Humanities Research Board) and the ESRC. There are programmes that involve natural and social scientists such as the Rural Economy and Land Use Programme (RELU). In this case ESRC is a provider of

---

Box 7.2 Websites of research councils and private foundations funding research

Arts and Humanities Research Council (AHRC)	www.ahrc.ac.uk
British Academy	www.britac.ac.uk
Carnegie Trust	www.carnegietrust.org.uk
Economic and Social Research Council (ESRC)	www.esrc.ac.uk
Ford Foundation	www.fordfound.org
Joseph Rowntree Foundation (JRF)	www.jrf.org.uk
Leverhulme Trust	www.leverhulme.org.uk
Nuffield Foundation	www.nuffieldfoundation.org
Volkswagen Foundation	www.volkswagen-stiftung.de
Wellcome Trust	www.wellcome.ac.uk

funds alongside the biological and natural environment research councils. The different operating procedures of the different research councils are not easily reconcilable, and researchers may be challenged by unfamiliar forms developed for natural science projects. The AHRC collaborates with the Engineering and Physical Sciences Research Council (EPSRC) in a Designing for the 21st Century Programme that attempts to develop new partnerships across the arts and physical sciences to enhance understanding of creativity in design and the development of novel design applications. However, although multidisciplinary work is expected to be more common in the future, most young researchers are unlikely to encounter challenges of this kind. It should be noted that all the research councils now use an electronic submission system known as Je-S, which has replaced paper submissions. If you intend to make an application to a research council, you need to register with Je-S and familiarize yourself with its requirements and operating procedures. Early indications are that this system is far from easy to operate, and some training from your university's research support services is essential.

The AHRC uses a liberal interpretation of its subject domain in the arts and humanities, and there are some areas of overlap with the work of the ESRC, for example, in relation to the study of philosophy. Like the ESRC, the AHRC has both responsive mode schemes and strategic initiatives. The former schemes allow researchers to propose projects in their own areas of research interest and are often more suitable for younger researchers. The latter involve the identification of strategic research priorities by the AHRC where it is thought that a concerted research effort is necessary. The ESRC decided in 2005 to increase funding of responsive grants, including a new responsive large grants scheme for research groups, networks and projects. ESRC's objective is to increase the responsive grants success rate from 20 per cent in 2005 to 25 per cent in 2010. The ESRC also introduced a First Grants Scheme to assist new researchers at the start of their careers in gaining experience of managing and leading research projects. The first call closed in January 2006. It was expected to support up to 20 awards, and further calls are expected.

In the cases of both the AHRC and ESRC, being involved in a research initiative or programme has advantages and disadvantages. You know in advance that a usually substantial sum of money has been allocated for research in a particular area. You will have the opportunity to work alongside researchers with similar interests, whom you will join in workshops and other events linked to the programme, allowing you to develop your personal networks. You will be able to meet and make your work known to some of the leading researchers in your area. You will gain valuable knowledge about new theoretical, methodological and empirical developments in area of interest to you.

However, despite the good intentions of the research councils and the programme organizers, research programmes can often bring together people with very disparate interests and divergent or even conflicting intellectual agendas. The effort to impose some coherence on the programme as a whole can lead the person designated to organize the programme to be quite interventionist in your research. Not all the meetings or workshops you will be expected to attend are necessarily relevant or helpful. Nevertheless, it is possible to apply for small grants within a programme, and if you are successful, your work may be brought to the attention of key academics who can further your career.

The AHRC's Research Grant scheme provides for grants of up to £500,000 over five years, although most grants are for smaller amounts and shorter durations. The Research Leave scheme funds replacement teaching costs for three or four months so that scholars can complete a research project, but requires a matching contribution by the employing institution. Innovation awards of up to £50,000 are available for projects that challenge existing models, perceptions or modes of thought. There is a small grant scheme of up to £5000 for the creative and performing arts.

The ESRC provides research grants of between £15,000 and £1.5 million. The lower limit means there are some pieces of work that would be too small scale for the ESRC, and funding could more appropriately be sought from charitable foundations. It should be noted, however, that the ESRC welcomes applications for scoping studies that are intended to enable researchers to assess and demonstrate the feasibility of a project. Proposals of over £100,000 are treated as part of the large grants scheme and are sent to five referees, one of whom is nominated by the applicant. The application is then graded by the members of the Research Grants Board. The small grants scheme is more suitable for new researchers making their first application to the ESRC. A member of the Research Grants Board and one member of the ESRC's Virtual Research College will assess the application. Funding decisions are usually made within 14 weeks, compared with 24 weeks for large grants.

The ESRC also offers a research fellowship scheme that is open to less experienced as well as senior researchers to undertake a period of concentrated research activity. Funding for fellowships is being increased following the strategic review published in December 2005. Fellowships last for two years, and a programme of work has to be specified rather than a single research project. The awards are intended to develop the careers of outstanding researchers, but an award can be based on research potential as well as a track record of excellence. There are special provisions for mentoring and career development for researchers with less than ten years' experience. Clearly these awards are very attractive, and hence highly competitive, but obtaining one would serve as a major boost to a young researcher's career.

The ESRC's Research Seminars Competition has attracted considerable interest. Up to £15,000 can be made available to a group for a programme of seminars lasting up to two years. Particular encouragement is given to seminar groups designed to bring together researchers from different disciplines to identify new research agendas. Becoming involved in one of these seminar groups is an excellent way for young researchers to develop new contacts and improve their access to new ideas.

The British Academy receives grant-in-aid from the government Office of Science and Technology to fund research in all branches of the humanities and social sciences. Its programmes are of particular value to younger researchers as it emphasizes small-scale support and responsive rather than directive modes of funding. The Academy runs a small research grants scheme with a maximum grant of £7500 over two years. The eligible costs are quite broadly defined to include travel and maintenance, research assistance, workshops, consumables, specialist software and the cost of interpreters in the field. The grants do not cover computer hardware, replacement teaching costs or attendance at conferences, for which purpose the British Academy has a distinct Conference Grants Scheme. There are three closing dates a year for small research grants, so applicants should not be constrained by immediate deadlines, although it takes three months to reach a decision.

The Academy has a larger research grants scheme, which provides maximum funding of £20,000 over three years. This is only £5000 above the ESRC's minimum limit, and the Academy emphasizes that grants are not intended to support the employment of a full-time research assistant for 12 months. Applicants with staff-rich projects are advised to apply to the AHRC or ESRC. Nevertheless, this is an attractive scheme for a medium-sized project that could follow on from a researcher's initial smaller-scale project. One drawback is that there is just one application date a year, in October, although at least this gives time over the summer vacation to prepare an application. It also takes five months to reach a decision.

Charitable foundations

Charitable foundations, often established by a single rich benefactor whose name is in their title, have substantial sums of money at their disposal that their trust deeds require them to spend on research each year. For example, the Leverhulme Trust spends £25 million a year on research. In many ways, the private foundations are relatively benign funders. They intrude less into research than public funders, and may be less insistent on a dialogue with 'stakeholders', 'users' and 'practitioners' which, although useful in some respects, can distort research objectives and delay completion. They are more open to projects critical of government policy (Barnes, 1979, p. 79). They may also be more flexible in their assessment of outcomes, being more willing to engage in a subjective evaluation of whether the project has tackled issues that matter, rather than how many articles in leading refereed journals have resulted from it. The Ford Foundation states, 'Ford staff members understand that the work the foundation and its grantees undertake together is difficult, that success often results from multiple efforts over a long period, and that setbacks are likely' (http://www. fordfound.org/about/guideline.cfm?print_version=1, 10 June 2005). It should be emphasized, however, that there the ratio of unsuccessful to successful applications can be high, so these are not necessarily easier routes to obtain funds than the research councils. The Ford Foundation awarded just 5 per cent (2091) of the 41,000 grant applications it received in 2004 (http://www.fordfound.org/about/guideline.cfm?print_version=1, 10 June 2005).

Although the principal focus in this section will be on UK foundations, it is worth noting that funding may be obtained for suitable projects from overseas foundations. Apart from the Gulbenkian Foundation based in Portugal, the wealthiest European foundation is the VolkswagenStiftung or Volkswagen Foundation, which provides funding of about €100 million a year for research. Part of its mission is to provide support for aspiring young scholars, and it places a particular emphasis on interdisciplinary research. The Foundation's work is structured around funding initiatives such as intellectual foundations and requirements for a new Europe, but once an initiative has achieved its purpose of generating new ideas it is replaced by a new one. Provided a project falls under one of the current funding initiatives and involves substantial cooperation with researchers in Germany, applications are invited from academic institutions located outside Germany.

Of the American foundations, the largest is the Ford Foundation, although its global network of offices does not cover Europe. This in part reflects its focus on advancing human welfare by making grants to develop new ideas or strengthen key organizations that address poverty and injustice, and also promote democratic values, international cooperation and human achievement. Programmes in 2005 included governance and civil society; education, sexuality and religion; and media, arts and culture.

Charitable foundations whose main focus appears in the natural sciences may nevertheless provide funding for research in the humanities and social sciences. The Wellcome Trust is a leading funder of medical research, spending as much as the government's own body, the Medical Research Council. However, its work spills over into the humanities and natural sciences. Among the topics it covers are subjects of interest to philosophers, historians and public policy analysts, including work in medical ethics, the history of medicine and public awareness of medical developments. Its support for the history of medicine is vital for that specialist area, which it defines broadly, and it has a very wide and flexible array of grants ranging from project grants to schemes for research expenses and travel grants. It also has a scheme to attract outstanding research staff in early to mid-career, providing support for a post for five years, which is then converted to a permanent position in the recipient university.

The following discussion considers UK charitable foundations that fund research across disciplines within either the social sciences or the social sciences and humanities. It is worth bearing in mind that some smaller foundations with more specific objectives may be useful funding sources. For example, the Alcohol Education and Research Council (AERC) funds four or five projects a year costing around £50,000 each.

The most important private foundation in the UK is the Leverhulme Trust. It supports research in all fields except social policy and welfare, medicine and school education. The funding it provides that is of interest to younger researchers is focused on research projects with an emphasis on paying for research assistants, linked postgraduate and modest direct support costs. It rarely pays for replacement teaching costs. There is a two-stage application process, with an outline application being submitted first. Applications for over £250,000 are more elaborate, and may sometimes involve visits and discussions with the applicant.

The Nuffield Foundation provides grants for social scientists, and two of its schemes are of particular interest to younger researchers. The New Career Development Fellowships Scheme is not a conventional postdoctoral fellowship schemes, but offers high-flying social scientists in the early stages of their career a chance to take a change of direction, for example through acquiring a substantive new body of knowledge or an additional methodology. It involves a collaborative partnership between a younger social scientist and someone who is more established and experienced, who is expected to be actively engaged in the fellow's intellectual development. The Social Science Small Grants Scheme has been the first step on the research grants ladder for many early career researchers and is ideal for smaller self-contained, pilot or preliminary projects. The maximum award is normally £7500 and applications can be made at any time.

Two foundations are particularly concerned with research that is likely to impact policy and practice. The Joseph Rowntree Foundation (JRF) has been an important funder of social research broadly conceived: for example on poverty, housing, immigration, parenting, and drugs and alcohol. The Carnegie UK Trust has a particular interest in larger-scale action research designed to change public policy. It has switched its emphasis from reactive short-term grants to supporting longer-term programmes such as that on social problems in rural areas. The Anglo-German Foundation provides around £40,000 each year for small research projects or to meet the costs of seminars and workshops, with a ceiling for small grants of £4000.

Government departments and the European Union

Government departments have a number of drawbacks as research sponsors. They often work to relatively tight timetables and there will be no leeway for late delivery. They also expect research to answer very specific questions, and they will not be slow to express their displeasure if they do not get the answers they want. They may also have a preference for quantitative measures, and there are relatively few opportunities for researchers from the humanities. Support is sometimes given to syntheses or state of the art surveys that review existing research. These are useful exercises, but unlikely to give the researcher as much credit as original research. On the other hand, researchers who establish a good reputation with a department may find it relatively easy to obtain research funding. It is also an attractive option for researchers who are interested in engaging in a dialogue with policy makers and want to see their research have an impact on policy decisions.

The Department of Environment, Food and Rural Affairs (Defra) is a major sponsor of research, spending around £155 million a year. Much of this is devoted to natural science research, but programmes such as that for sustainable rural communities offer opportunities for social scientists. Defra operates a two-stage application process, with a short form known as a 'statement of interest' being used to short list applicants for the final round. The Department for International Development's (DFID) Central Research Department plans to spend £100 million a year on research in 2006–7, offering considerable opportunities for social scientists. Its eight development research centres are consortia involving developing countries, which run five-year policy research programmes. Another major government funder is the Home Office. It has a large in-house research operation, but also commissions a substantial amount of external research work in areas that are of particular interest to criminologists and sociologists.

Foreign governments can be a useful source of funding for short research visits. The German Academic Exchange Service (Deutscher Akademischer Austausch Dienst, DAAD) operates on a philosophy of 'people before projects'. Its most important programme for foreign researchers is one that enables them to come to Germany for research stays of between one and three months, primarily to carry out their own research work in cooperation with the German colleagues who issued the invitation.

The Canadian government provides generous support for Canadian Studies in Britain, which is available to a wide range of disciplines. Faculty Research Program Awards are for the purpose of enabling short-term research about Canada or on aspects of Canada's bilateral relations with the UK, leading to the publication of an article in a learned journal in the UK. The award is up to a maximum value of C$4000 to cover the cost of a transatlantic flight and subsistence for up to five weeks in Canada. Institutional Research Program Awards are designed for major team research about Canada, comparative Canada–UK topics, or on aspects of Canada's relations with the UK, leading to the publication of a research monograph. There is an annual application deadline, currently 31 October.

The European Union is an extensive research sponsor, particularly for the social sciences. Application procedures for EU grants are particularly onerous, despite repeated assurances that they will be streamlined. Monitoring and reporting arrangements can also be demanding. They are certainly not a suitable funding route for young researchers operating on their own initiative, and many senior researchers have become disillusioned with the transaction costs involved in making an application to the European Union, which often seems hardly worth it even if an award is made. However, if an opportunity to participate in an EU programme becomes available it is worth considering if only for the network of contacts it will give you throughout Europe.

The European Union's main form of support for research is through framework programmes (FP), which are organized around a set of themes. More information is available at the European Union's CORDIS website (http://www.cordis.lu/en/home.html) and from the Department of Trade and Industry (http://fp6uk.ost.gov.uk). FP6 has a budget of €19 billion over the period 2002–6. Research applications have to come from two member states and usually from more, so a substantial part of the application process is building the network of researchers and making sure that they provide all the necessary information in the required form. In the past the chances of an application succeeding were undoubtedly enhanced if a southern member state was involved, and in the current period it is helpful to have participants from at least one of the accession states. Proposals were announced in April 2005 for FP7, which will run from 2007 to 2013. These proposals include a thematic heading for socio-economic sciences and the humanities, which is intended to encourage collaborative research that draws on Europe's strong research base in the humanities and social sciences. However, it is evident that the research is intended to address socio-economic issues rather than more traditional humanities themes.

The European Union's COST (a French abbreviation for European Cooperation in the field of Scientific and Technical Research) scheme is a useful mechanism for building networks of European researchers who can then go on to apply to FPs or undertake other forms of collaborative research. From the European Union's perspective, COST is intended to provide scientific input to the policy-making process rather than facilitate academic research. However, the arrangements for the former seem patchy at best, while the latter often works well. Once again considerable coordination costs fall on the organizers, but as a participant you will receive travel and subsistence funding to attend meetings of the network. The main focus of COST is on the natural sciences, however, with the social sciences and humanities being a subordinate grouping within one of the three clusters of staff in the COST office.

It is evident from this survey that rather more funding is available for social scientists than for researchers in the humanities. Social science projects can be more expensive because they use surveys and large data sets. Much humanities research requires relatively small grants for travel and subsistence, although this also applies to some qualitative work in the social sciences. Researchers in both sets of disciplines are likely to find themselves under more pressure to undertake research that recovers FEC for their universities.

▶ Ethical considerations

All research projects involving human participants raise ethical issues, and these are becoming of increasing concern to both universities and research councils. Most universities now have ethics committees which function as research gatekeepers, and whose approval you have to seek before undertaking or securing funding for research. The precise arrangements will vary from one university to another, but will usually involve the submission of a standard form for consideration by the committee. This may pose greater problems for social scientists than for humanities academics, as the former are often involved in quite interventionist forms of research which impinge on citizens, whereas the latter may be concerned with events or persons from the past (although tricky data protection issues may arise in relation to the use of archives).

The broad issues that arise may include dependent relationships between researcher and subject and their possible exploitation; protection from harm; and rights to withdraw. Considerable emphasis is usually placed on the doctrine of informed consent when undertaking research that involves human subjects. This is generally understood to mean a process by which a research subject understands the nature and consequences of participating in research, has a free choice about participating and can withdraw from the research. It is a principle that originates in medical research, where its application may be more straightforward than in social research. The confidentiality of information supplied by research subjects and the anonymity of respondents need to be respected. Particular care is needed when research involves vulnerable groups in society. More generally, potential risks and harm to participants need to be identified. Any risks to those undertaking the research also need to be identified and means of minimizing and monitoring them explained.

Box 7.3 Research councils' terms and conditions on research ethics

The Research Organisation is responsible for ensuring that ethical issues relevant to the research project are identified and brought to the attention of the relevant approval or regulatory body. Approval to undertake the research must be granted before any work requiring approval begins. Ethical issues should be interpreted broadly and may encompass, among other things, the involvement of human participants in research, the use of animals, research that may result in damage to the environment and the use of sensitive economic, social or personal data.

Source: Arts and Humanities Research Council.

The research councils have a single set of core terms and conditions which include a paragraph on research ethics, which is reproduced in Box 7.3. The ESRC insists that 'Applicants should demonstrate that full consideration has been given to the ethical implications of their research, and justify their means of resolving the ethical issues arising' (http://www.esrcsocietytoday.ac.uk/ESRCInfo-Centre/Support/research_award_holders, 13 June 2005). The ESRC has an Ethics Advisory Board to which it may refer applications for advice on ethical issues. In 2005 the ESRC published a new Research Ethics Framework based on six key principles, which will be mandatory for all applications to the research council from January 2006 (see Box 7.4).

Applicants to the ESRC are encouraged to refer to the codes of ethics of professional associations. A code with wide applicability in the social sciences is that of the Social Research Association (http://www.the-sra.org.uk). The European Commission has also been drawing up a set of professional guidelines for the conduct of socio-economic research known as the RESPECT Code of Practice (http://www.respectproject.org). This is based on a synthesis of a large number of existing professional and ethical codes of practice. This code is based on three underlying principles: upholding scientific standards, compliance with the law, and avoidance of social and personal harm. The code recognizes that there are no universal principles that allow an unambiguous judgement about the ethical merits of a particular research proposal. Indeed, 'Carrying out socio-economic research in a professional and ethical manner involves

---

Box 7.4 ESRC Research Ethics Framework

The framework sets out six key principles:

- Research should be designed, reviewed and undertaken to ensure integrity and quality.
- Research staff and subjects must be informed fully about the purpose, methods and intended possible uses of the research, what their participation in the research involves, methods and intended possible uses of the research and what risks, if any, are involved.
- The confidentiality of information supplied by research subjects and the anonymity of respondents must be respected.
- Research participants must participate in a voluntary way, free from any coercion.
- Harm to research participants must be avoided.
- The independence of research must be clear, and any conflicts of interest or partiality must be explicit.

Source: *Social Science*, 60, June 2005, p. 14.

---

balancing a number of different principles which often lie in tension with each other' (http://www.respectproject.org/code/index.php, 13 June 2005).

Indeed, the ESRC states that it has an obligation 'to ensure that the research which it funds will not give rise to distress or annoyance to individuals'. The problem this raises is that genuinely innovative or thought-provoking research may well annoy individuals or groups in society, and such annoyance might actually be part of a process of social change. There is a need to maintain a balance between the costs of research to particular groups and the benefits it brings to society as a whole. There is a risk that university ethics committees in particular may be reluctant to support research that is embarrassing or awkward, or may involve the institution in controversy, regardless of its wider value. The problem of balancing a proper attention to ethical considerations with a defence of the autonomy and independence of research raises issues that go beyond the scope of this book. The entry researcher needs to be aware of these issues and of their importance, and to develop the ability to build into the research a proper appreciation of ethical principles that will satisfy research sponsors without compromising the objectives of the research itself.

▶ Managing a research grant

Once the excitement of securing a research grant has subsided, you need to think carefully about how you are going to manage the grant so that you can secure your own goals and provide the outcomes you have promised the research sponsor. Careful planning of the research at the application stage will, of course, help you in this task. It is understandable that many academics focus on the research objectives and how they will be achieved, and devote less attention to the budget and logistics of the research. These will become more important as the research gets under way.

Managing a research grant is another aspect of being an academic where time management skills are very important. In larger projects, there will be 'deliverables' and 'milestones', and you will be expected to deliver an annual report on progress. However, even in smaller projects devices like a Gantt chart can be a helpful means of reminding you when particular phases of the research activity have to be started and completed. This is a horizontal bar graph where the horizontal axis is a timescale, normally starting from the beginning of the project and most typically expressed in months. Rows of bars, which will often overlap, show the beginning and ending dates of individual tasks and activities in the research project. When undertaking activities like interviewing, it is important to allow enough time for making contact with respondents and setting up the interview. Particular care with forward planning is necessary when interviews are to be undertaken abroad during a limited time period.

The task of managing the research budget will normally be helped by regular statements of income and expenditure from the relevant unit within the university finance or research and grants office. 'The key to managing research ... budgets is to make sure that all of the money allocated, or almost all, is spent, but no more' (Blaxter, Hughes and Tight, 1998, p. 130). If you overspend, the money will have to be found from somewhere. It will not usually be your own pocket, unless there is gross negligence, but your head of department will not be pleased about having to dip into departmental funds to make up the shortfall. Equally, any unspent money will have to be returned to the sponsor and may raise questions about your ability to plan and execute the financial aspects of a research project. Managing the finances of a research project is not straightforward, as costs, particularly non-wage costs, may vary over the lifetime of the project. Travel costs are particularly difficult to control because they may fluctuate unexpectedly, particularly in relation to foreign travel. It is important to retain enough money to fund additional interviews or archive visits towards the end of the project.

Managing staff, even if they are only working for you on a part-time or on a casual basis, can be one of the most challenging aspects of running a research project. In all cases, it is important that both you and the staff member are clear about what the expectations are on each side in terms of workload and tasks. If you are appointing a research assistant, it is important to check that he or she has all the skills relevant to the project, or can acquire them relatively easily and quickly. If foreign language skills are required, a test should be organized as part of the appointment process. The standard appointment procedures and checklists of human resources departments should help to identify relevant skills and ensure that they are met. Research assistants need to demonstrate that they can work as a member of the team and, while bringing particular skills and perspectives to the project, should not seek to impose their own agenda on it.

It is necessary to be particularly careful if you are funding part of the time of a support staff member who also has other duties. It is important to have a clear understanding with the head of department or line manager about how time is to be allocated, so that sufficient time is set aside for your work. This can be quite complex when the workload varies at different stages of the project, and is a potential source of friction with other people with calls on the staff member's time who may think that their own work is being neglected. It might seem an attractive solution to build in additional hours for an existing clerical member of staff to your project, but if there is sufficient work, it might be better to appoint a new member of staff on a part-time basis who is dedicated to your project.

Ensure that you pay sufficient attention to the dissemination aspects of your project, which are becoming increasingly important to research sponsors. A well-designed website can help to publicize your project and can be a useful reference point for potential interviewees. Liaise with your university press and publicity office about media opportunities. Any workshops or other formal dissemination activities should be planned well in advance, and you should also make sure that you apply in time for any conferences where you want to make presentations from your project.

It is easy to become diverted into promising new lines of enquiry during your research. These may provide a useful basis for future research applications. However, always remember that you have undertaken to deliver specific results to your research sponsor. The end-of-grant report is an important way of demonstrating that you have met your research objectives, and the grades that you are awarded by research council referees in particular can affect your chances of success in future research applications. It has to be written at a time when you have perhaps become a little tired of the research project, and it may seem to be a less exciting document to write than research papers. It is, however, an important output and should not be composed in a hurry. One key objective in a research project must always be to remain on good terms with the research sponsor, to whom you may wish to apply again.

▶ Consultancy

Consultancy involves an academic using his or her expertise to offer advice for payment to a commercial purchaser, typically a firm, but it could be a government department, a university or an intermediary. The advice could be very specific, related to a particular problem faced by a firm or other institution, or it could be general contextual advice on economic or political developments. Business schools have placed a great emphasis on consultancy activities, and staff may be required to undertake them or encouraged to spend one day a week on them. This is in part because they are a means of raising revenue, but also because they provide a means of developing links with business and offer a means of demonstrating the practical applicability of the work under-taken in a business school. Social scientists in general are likely to have more opportunities for undertaking consultancy work than scholars in the humanities, although one of our respondents had provided consul-tancy to other universities on developing writing courses, and other opportunities arise more generally in the area of teaching and learning, particularly through the work of subject centres. The emphasis placed by government on developing links with industry, and the need to find new sources of university funds, have led to efforts to give a greater empha-sis to consultancy. Whether it will be recognized 'as a core activity along-side teaching and research' (*Times Higher Education Supplement*, 24 August 2001) remains to be seen.

Because consultancy work is undertaken for a client which hopes to obtain information or insights that will be of some value to it, the extent to which it can be published will usually be substantially constrained. Certainly, permission and clearance would be required from a firm where you had undertaken work, for example to advise it on its internal organizational structures. Consultancy work can be quite lucrative, but it can also detract from the time that you spend on academic forms of research, which might be more important for your longer-term career. Unless you are working in a business school, however, you are likely to be offered relatively few opportunities for consultancy in an early stage of your career. This is borne out by the young academics we interviewed, who reported very little experience of consultancy.

It may be more satisfactory to undertake work for an experienced intermediary that specializes in linking the academic world with commercial and government clients. Oxford Analytica (www.oxan.com) was set up in 1975 as an international, independent consulting firm drawing on a network of over 1000 senior faculty members at Oxford and other major universities around the world. It seeks to provide analysis of the implications of national and international developments facing corporations, banks, governments and international institutions, harnessing the expertise of academic experts to provide timely and authoritative analysis of world events. Oxford Analytica provides daily brief services to subscribers, which offer short analyses of contemporary issues, typically around 1200 words and following a standard format. It also undertakes more specific work for particular clients. Although it is possible to apply online to undertake work for it, most studies are commissioned and the work generally goes to academics with an established reputation.

There are some parallels between media work and consultancy work, although the latter is generally better paid. You must be able to meet very tight deadlines. You must also be able to communicate your knowledge in a way that can be understood by audiences that do not share your understanding. With media work you are, of course, communicating to anyone who can be bothered to watch, listen to or read what you are saying. Consultancy involves working for very exclusive or even unknown audiences, and this may raise conflicts of interest or ethical questions that concern you. You also need to make sure that you understand any university rules about declaring or seeking permission for consultancy work, and whether you have to pay an overhead to the university, which may diminish the financial returns. Like media work, not everyone is suited to consultancy, but for some academics it can be very rewarding intellectually and financially.

▶ Conclusions

Obtaining research grants and successfully completing the research funded by them is an increasingly important part of the academic career. Appointment criteria for more senior posts usually specify a track record in obtaining major grants and it can be a significant consideration in internal promotions. One of the key tensions in managing a research grant is fulfilling your own intellectual goals while also satisfying the research sponsor who may in turn want you to demonstrate that you have disseminated your findings to 'practitioners' and 'stakeholders'. All this work has to be undertaken within a framework that increasingly emphasizes ethical considerations.

As suggested in this chapter, the best way to start is with small-scale research grants or in partnership with a more experienced researcher. Both these routes will give you a practical awareness of the skills needed to obtain a research grant and to manage it successfully. Unless you are in a discipline where its practice is particularly emphasized, consultancy is usually best avoided until a later stage of your career, and even then it has to be approached with care.

While you will be under considerable pressure to obtain research funding, remember that maximizing it is not the same thing as optimizing it. A frenetic life in which you are obtaining the funding for a new research grant while still working on the last one is not an ideal one. Above all, remember that research funding is a means of achieving your intellectual goals rather than an end in itself.

8 Conclusions

It is hoped that the guidance offered in this book will help you to make a successful start to your career. Of course, a book of this kind can only make suggestions about good practice and hints about how you can work more effectively. The aspirations and goals of academics, and what constitutes a satisfactory and fulfilling career, can vary considerably. As Emma noted, 'There are different types of academics, some devote their life to it and it's a vocation and perhaps they don't have anything else in their life and they're quite happy with that.' Most of our respondents, however, wanted to maintain a balance in their life so that work didn't completely dominate. As Zoe commented, 'I don't want to reach the top at any cost.'

Long working hours can bring diminishing returns, and it is important to set periods of time aside in your life that allow you to move completely away from your work. Some academics, for example, like watching football because it takes you into a completely different milieu where emotion predominates over reason and success and failure is not in your hands, but can be blamed on the players, the manager or the match officials. Others may enjoy activities that appeal to an aesthetic sensibility such as visiting art galleries or going to the opera. The particular activity is less important than the fact that it is divorced from your normal academic activities. Hence, going to see a play is a different experience for a sociologist than for a lecturer in English. Whatever you do, it should involve an element of participation rather than being merely passive. You will then return refreshed and able to work more effectively.

It is also important to set aside time when you can reflect on your personal development and the extent to which you are achieving what you want to in your academic career. Academic life should allow for more time for reflection than most careers, but the increasing pressures from a variety of sources are eating away at the time when you can pause and reflect rather than simply tackle the most urgent task that faces you. However, if you don't set aside time to reflect, you will find yourself becoming increasingly reactive to goals and tasks set by others, rather than setting and pursuing your own intellectual agenda. 'Away days' are increasingly popular in universities, when departments or course teams reflect on what they have achieved and where they are going. Individuals need their own personal 'away days' when they can find time and space in a relaxing environment to reflect on their career development and their personal goals.

▶ Next steps in an academic career

This book has been principally concerned with the early years of an academic career. These early years are taken up with accustoming yourself to the rules and norms of academic life and carving out a reputation as a researcher and as a teacher and supervisor. They involve becoming familiar with what is necessary to publish in peer-reviewed journals, how to secure a book contract with a publisher, and how to secure and manage a research grant. It is to be hoped that you will acquire good habits of time management and the ability to inter-relate effectively with colleagues. However, as your career progresses, new opportunities and challenges will appear.

External examiner of a degree programme

For example, you may be asked to become the external examiner for an undergraduate or postgraduate degree or set of degrees. Despite efforts at standardization, the experience of being an external examiner still varies quite a lot from one programme and one university to another. It is a rather different experience being an external examiner for a post-graduate degree with a small intake as distinct from a large undergrad-uate programme offering a wide range of degrees, although large undergraduate programmes generally have more than one external examiner. In general, the role of the external examiner has been chang-ing. At one time, the external examiner would be expected to principally confine him or herself to approving examination papers, checking the standard of marking by reading a sample of work, and adjudicating on the work of marginal, disagreed, failing or first class candidates. These tasks remain, although many departments seek to resolve disagreements or marginal marks internally if they can, so that the external examiner just sees enough work to verify the standard of marking. However, as the role has changed, the external examiner is increasingly expected to comment on such matters as the objectives of the course, the content of the syllabus, and the way in which learning is provided.

External examining can be an interesting way of learning about the teaching methods and procedures of other departments and programmes, offering the opportunity to import good practice from elsewhere. It is also an opportunity to learn something about the strengths and weaknesses of the department itself, and it is not unknown for external examiners to be recruited to the staff of a department, if they have not been put off by what they have observed. Being offered the opportunity of being an external examiner of a degree programme is another milepost in an academic career, rather like being invited to be a PhD examiner for the first time. It is a sign that you are regarded as senior, experienced and trustworthy enough to undertake this important function, although it has to be said that given the reluctance of many senior staff to take on too many roles of this kind, departments are often desperate to recruit someone who meets their university's standards.

You should be warned that external examining can be very time-consuming, with the work arriving at a very busy time of year when you will probably be marking for your own institution. It is generally not particularly well paid, although again there are perplexing variations between programmes and institutions, with a variety of methods for calculating the appropriate payment. Because these are bound by university rules, it is generally not possible to negotiate a higher fee. At one time the arrival of the external examiner would be equivalent to a royal progress, with the individual concerned being accommodated at the university for a period of days and wined and dined. As exam boards have become increasingly businesslike, with outcomes increasingly determined by the application by rules rather than the exercise of discretion, and difficult medical or other personal cases screened beforehand, it is often possible to travel to the university concerned and back in one day. The entertainment has become correspondingly less lavish.

The most rewarding programmes to examine are small postgraduate degrees that have some relevance to your interests. You will generally be reading high-quality work from which you might learn something, and you will have the chance to talk to the experts in the area at the institution where you are examining. Because of the way in which examining fees are calculated, with a basic fee for examining a degree and attending the board, the financial rewards will probably be relatively good for the amount of work involved. At the other end of the spectrum is the large undergraduate degree that forms part of a complex network of programmes in a not particularly well-organized department. Large packets of scripts will arrive late on subjects in which you are not particularly interested. Many of the scripts will be indecipherable or of poor quality. There will be no clear instructions about what you are supposed to do with them in the time available. Of course, poor procedure is something that you can complain about as an examiner, but it often arises from the complexity and poor organization of the programme itself and is not easily resolved.

External examining is a professional obligation and is something that you can place on your CV. It is one of those aspects of academic life where you need to learn to say 'no', and the fact that you already have potentially conflicting obligations at another institution is an acceptable answer. Too much external examining can use up time that could be spent on other activities that will have a much greater impact on your chances of promotion.

Moving on

Emma noted, 'I've been in my current position for five years and that's quite a long time. It's perhaps changed my perceptions a little in the sense that I thought that "oh, you just move on every so often".' Whether and how often you move depends on how dissatisfied with your current situation and whether a better opportunity exists elsewhere.

Even if you do not have to move house, a change of job involves some transition costs as you get used to the new position, so you should think that the new job is appreciably better in various ways than your existing one to offset your transition costs. As you get older, the personal costs of a move will tend to increase, unless it is a geographical shift that locates you closer to a partner. Will your partner need to change job? How will the education of your children be affected? Will you be moving to an area where housing costs are higher? In some respects it may be easier to move earlier in a career, but that may be psychologically more difficult when you are still establishing yourself as an academic and in a department. If you move too often, you might get the reputation as someone who lacks commitment. As a rule of thumb, do not move until five years after your first permanent job, unless you are deeply dissatisfied with your existing position or a golden opportunity presents itself.

Another decision point is when you are approaching promotion to senior lecturer. Universities are understandably cautious and rigorous about internal promotions. This is partly because of a proper concern for maintaining standards. However, departments may also be concerned about disturbing the internal pecking order, although that may sometimes reflect a judgement about solid achievement and a willingness to undertake tiresome tasks rather than how the candidates would be ranked externally. Applying for a job elsewhere might help to concentrate their minds, but it is a job offer from elsewhere that usually produces action as distinct from vague promises of future preferment. You should therefore only apply for jobs where you have a real chance of success, and which are really attractive to you, if your real aim is to secure internal promotion. Think in advance about how you would react to an offer of a readership from a university elsewhere with somewhat more money compared with a senior lectureship in an existing institution. Applying for jobs elsewhere, obtaining them and then not accepting them, if done too often, might damage your internal as well as your external reputation.

Don't feel that you are obliged to move on at regular intervals. You do not have to do so for reasons of intellectual challenge or stimulation, because that may come from new recruits to your own department (try to ensure that you have an influence on new appointments as you become more senior), academics in other departments in your own university, or, most importantly, from your developing network of international contacts. Equally, if there is a department or unit that has an outstanding reputation in your area of expertise and you are invited to join it, it would be foolish to refuse. However, staying in one place does not mean that you necessarily become intellectually stale. There may be good reasons for staying in a successful university and department that has a good location and attracts excellent students. Equally, if the university and department appear to be failing, or are in a city that is remote and unattractive and attracts poor students, there is a good case for seeking a new job. Most situations fall between these polar extremes and, as in all important career decisions, you need to carefully assess the pros and cons of moving. The final decision may, however, be made on the basis of intuition, and once you have assessed all the relevant considerations carefully, it is not a bad thing to do whatever feels right.

Later in your career, if you are interested in maximizing your income as a primary goal, it is probably a good idea to move. With the abolition of the professorial average, six-figure salaries for professors in the humanities and social sciences are not unknown. They are rarely a reward for loyalty to an institution but are used to attract academic stars who may also receive a 'golden hello' in the form of reduced teaching hours, enhanced research funds and extended study leave. Such benefits are not available, however, to relatively new entrants.

Management

Every new entrant will be expected to take on some administrative tasks in his or her department, and this will become progressively more onerous as probation is left behind. Tasks such as an admissions officer, examinations secretary or programme director can be especially demanding of time at particular periods of the year. Being an admissions officer, for example, means that you have to be available at the time A level results are announced. You will also finding yourself dealing with emails, phone calls and letters from parents and teachers. In some universities, there is an increasing effort to transfer many of these tasks to academic administrators so that academics are left free to concentrate on teaching and research.

At some point, however, you will be faced with the challenge of becoming an academic manager rather than just carrying out administrative tasks. Quite what the distinction is between administration and management could be the subject of a book by itself. In practice, 'management' is often used as a more fashionable way to describe tasks that used to be referred to as 'administration'. For the purposes of this book, administration is seen as applying already established rules to particular cases: for example, the application of examination conventions to a set of marks by an examinations secretary. Management involves decisions about the allocation of resources, whether human or financial, to achieve specified goals. It entails choosing between alternative courses of action or sometimes taking the more difficult but better choice of doing nothing. A head of department can usually be regarded as a line manager. Whether a deputy head could be so categorized would depend on his or her tasks and responsibilities.

Most of our respondents were unenthusiastic about the prospect of taking on management tasks at some point in their career. Zoe reflected a general view when she said, 'It doesn't really appeal to me.' Ruth pointed out, 'I think middle management is the worst management, or the worst tier of a management structure to be in.' Respondents who were more interested in the possibilities of a management route in their future career were all in post-1992 universities and excluded those respondents who anticipated a future move to an older university. Amy, who had had the experience of running her own centre, commented: 'I'm not afraid of it. You get a lot more perks and the chance to do something good as well.' Ian was attracted by the opportunity to influence what happened. Both Maria and Craig saw a clear academic management route to career advancement, which was perhaps more clearly mapped out in post-1992 universities. Craig reflected:

> There's a career route that's based around successful research that ends up with a professorship and other than that there is just the administrative and managerial route. The research route is increasingly difficult. I don't rule a management position out because I'm aware of the limited opportunities for furthering one's career in academia. I would probably not see it as my first choice, but it's a strong possibility.

Management may appear less attractive when it is contemplated than when it is actually undertaken. Academics have a reputation of being particularly difficult to manage, hence the frequent use of the phrase 'herding cats'. Some of them seem to see themselves as independent contractors who are provided with salaries and support services by their employers simply to pursue their own particular interests, regardless of the requirements of the institution or its students. The independence, autonomy and distinctiveness of cats make them attractive pets, and similar qualities help to define academics, but also make coordinating and directing their activities difficult. However, it is possible to develop relevant skills through experience, training and continuing professional development, even if the concept of 'leadership' is essentially contested, especially among academics (see Middlehurst, 1995).

Academics who have served as heads of departments generally find it difficult to keep up with research, or even if they are able to continue to produce focused research outputs, they find it difficult to set aside time for the reading that is necessary if they are to keep up with new developments in their discipline. As a consequence, after a while their effectiveness as researchers, and also as teachers, starts to decline. Undertaking a management position for a few years (and the tendency is for the terms of heads of department and other line management positions to become longer, say five years) is compatible with returning to a career as a researcher and teacher, but at some point you will face a decision about whether to specialize as a manager or as a researcher and teacher. If your skills and preferences lie in the direction of management, perhaps it would have been better to pursue a career as a university administrator in the first place. However, there are many high-level academic management posts that are effectively largely open only to those who can show a track record as successful academics. These include such posts as vice-chancellor, deputy or pro-vice-chancellor, faculty deans and a variety of positions in the research councils and foundations. A research project by Deem on new managerialism in universities has explored the roles adopted by manager-academics and their dispositions and the literature that has emerged from it is worth exploring for those interested in this aspect of career development (Deem, 2003a and 2003b).

It is quite legitimate, after a successful academic career, to aspire to a senior management post in academic life. The qualities that make you a good academic are, however, not necessarily the same as those of a good manager. Just as the most successful football managers have often not been outstanding players, so the best academic managers have not always been outstanding research academics or renowned teachers. The requirements of a senior academic management post can vary considerably, but will usually include at least the following:

- The ability to distinguish the strategically important issues and to develop a plan for tackling them.
- The ability to put that plan into effect by building coalitions of support for change, not easy in universities where staff are often highly change-resistant and there are multiple veto points.
- A good judge of individuals and their strengths and weaknesses, who can relate effectively to all sorts of people and persuade them to do what the institution wants.
- An understanding of current government higher education policy and likely developments in that policy.
- Excellent communication skills.
- Considerable stamina and the ability to deal with a wide range of issues simultaneously, seeing what is at the heart of each of them and avoiding the trap of becoming a micro manager.
- The ability to withstand the criticism that a change agent necessarily attracts, while retaining the ability to listen and take account of constructive criticism.

It is evident that relatively few people have such a combination of qualities, and those that have them may find more lucrative outlets for their talents than university management. Senior management positions in universities attract much higher salaries than those of even the best-paid professors (the ratio of the salaries of vice-chancellors to professors has increased considerably over the years). There may also be other perks in terms of comfortable travel arrangements and generous provision of support staff, while vice-chancellors are usually provided with accommodation. However, the real attraction of such a position is the chance to make a difference, to shape the development of an institution so that it responds effectively to new challenges and opportunities. It will, however, mean working very long hours, dealing with difficult individuals and attending some very dreary and frustrating meetings.

Occasionally one thinks that a younger colleague may have the potential to be a senior academic manager, but whether that potential is realized depends on that person's own preferences and chance life events. As your career develops, you should think about whether you would be interested in a senior academic management position and whether you have the necessary qualities. It is certainly not the right sort of position for someone who has a good analytical mind but is a poor judge of people or unable to take a decision. It requires an ability to assess a complex situation, to absorb advice and then to make a decision that can actually secure the desired outcome. It requires considerable resilience because you need to be able to ride out unpopularity and to have the ability to take decisions that are harsh but necessary for the success of the institution as a whole. If you have the right qualities, then you should think about making use of them, because universities need effective senior managers who nevertheless understand what the underlying purposes are of academic life.

▶ Is an academic career still worthwhile?

Our respondents were generally very positive about an academic career. It was significant that they found it difficult to respond to the questions about what had been their biggest mistake and their worst experience. They found it much easier to identify their best experience and their smartest move. As Luke recalled, he had done 'Nothing serious enough to be designated as a mistake. I think that the moves I've made have been reasonably smart.' In so far as our respondents had complaints, it was about the state of the market for academic jobs rather than the job itself. Once they had achieved a permanent position, our respondents were broadly satisfied with what they had experienced. For those in established posts, academic positions are still relatively secure compared with working in the private sector.

Of course, we were not interviewing a representative sample of academics. Our study has not captured those people who dropped out when undertaking their PhDs, gave up in despair after a succession of temporary posts or were surviving in a casual market in which they have had to make a living out of various part-time teaching posts, which lead them to live a marginalized experience. Nevertheless, our interviews illustrated the fact that not only is it possible to survive the pressures of contemporary academic life, it is possible to succeed and have a career that is enjoyable and fulfilling.

This is not to say that every day in academic life will be fulfilling, rewarding and enjoyable. It can be disheartening to deal with a poor examination script or essay from a module at which you have really worked hard, or to read a dismissive or sarcastic comment from a student in a feedback questionnaire. There will be dreary meetings to attend, apparently pointless forms to complete, difficult colleagues to deal with and the shock of rejection of an article you have been work-ing on for months or the publication of an unfavourable book review. Academic life is not for everyone and not all entrants will have a successful career, but as Zoe commented:

> I wouldn't try to put somebody off taking an academic career so long as they are aware that for a large number of people it isn't all ivory towers and nice wine cellars in old colleges. There is a lot of day-to-day stuff, a lot of paperwork. If you're not a 9 to 5 person it's certainly something to consider because it has as one of its benefits flexibility in terms of hours that you work.

Considerable publicity has been given to the problem of stress in academic life. Stress can have its positive aspects. A life that was entirely free of stress might also be free of any stimulating challenges. Enervation is not a desirable outcome. Some of the most stressful jobs are those that are repetitive and monotonous and often badly paid. Young academics today face more pressures than earlier generations, but they also receive more systematic support and training to prepare them for those challenges, whether it takes the form of teaching certifi-cates, mentoring, short courses or induction training. It is not so long ago that being an academic was a craft where you learnt norms and skills from an older generation, with much dependent on the talents of your mentor in conveying to you what the craft entailed. It was often assumed that white males from 'good' schools were best able to assim-ilate the relevant values and replicate them. The academic profession of today is more systematically organized, so that less is open to chance and, in principle at least, it should be more open to diversity. Nevertheless, it has been argued that 'There is more than enough evidence that stress in academia is rising faster than in other occupations and is having an impact on every aspect of life, from the lecture theatre to the bedroom' (Tytherleigh and Cooper, 2003).

There is survey evidence that suggests that 'Staff in new universities are more likely to suffer from stress and to become ill as a result than their counterparts in old institutions (*Times Higher Education Supplement*, 18 March 2005). This may reflect research pressures on top of a heavy teaching load and poor staff–student ratios, along with poor workload management. Nevertheless, competitive pressures in the wider economy are influencing all kinds of workplaces. A survey for the charity Common Purpose found that ambitious young people aged between 25 and 35 felt trapped at work, with nearly half (48 per cent) of the 1000 interviewed admitting that they felt stuck in their current jobs, with 56 per cent staying to pay off debts. Of those interviewed, 87 per cent were seeking careers that fulfilled their potential at work as well as adding purpose to their lives, but 59 per cent admitted that their jobs didn't fulfil their wider life ambitions (Frean, 2004).

The Common Purpose study supplemented its survey by focus group work, and some of the themes that emerged would not apply to young academics. For example, there were complaints about being 'stuck in a job that does not relate to their life ambitions' or 'not stretched or challenged enough at work'. These were not concerns that emerged from our discussions with our respondents. It may be that 'Britain's long-hours culture ... disproportionately impinges on higher education staff' (Tytherleigh and Cooper, 2003). Young academics need to learn to say no to additional duties, and universities need to create structures and systems of support that enable them to say no.

Appropriately qualified support staff who can undertake routine academically related tasks are a necessity rather than a luxury, and information technology services, often treated too much as an add-on in universities rather than a core integral function, need to be designed to enable staff to undertake tasks more efficiently and expeditiously. Nevertheless, when academics work long hours, it is because they are enthused about what they are doing. There is much truth in May's observation (2001, p. x) about 'those who would castigate their positions while conveniently forgetting the opportunities [academic life] has afforded them and more importantly, what it might afford others whose enthusiasm and abilities await those same opportunities'. There are few careers that are intellectually stimulating, and offer you the opportunity to develop the potential of others and to contribute through the power of ideas to bring about social change and a better society.

This book has suggested that there are some useful techniques that academic entrants can apply in such areas as teaching and time management, skills that help us to be effective supervisors, and that there is useful information to be absorbed about how to get published or win a research grant. Above all, it is important to strive for quality in everything you do, without being so perfectionist that you cannot cope.

Definitions of what constitute success vary, and there are different paths to it for each person, although they may cover common terrain. Serendipity can play an important role. In Wyn Grant's case, an early experience of journalism gave him an interest in politics and an ability to write effectively under pressure. The first job he applied for happened to be at Warwick, which was not then a well-regarded university, but became a very successful one. Anyone can float upwards on a rising tide, but you need to be aware of obstacles and risks that may impede or halt your progress. Above all, be true to yourself and your own values. As Shakespeare wrote:

> Our doubts are traitors,
> And make us lose the good we oft might win
> By fearing to attempt.
>
> (Measure for Measure)

Asked for one piece of advice for a new entrant, Ruth said:

> To keep hold of the intellectual reasons why you entered the profession in the first place. There is a lot about meeting the institutional requirements – do not let it grind you down, as it does not seem to make much difference to your career development. The only thing that makes it worthwhile is pursuing the ideas that brought you into this job.

References

Atkinson, M. (2004) *Lend Me Your Ears* (London: Vermilion).

Barnes, J. A. (1979) *Who Should Know What? Social Science, Privacy and Ethics* (Harmondsworth: Penguin).

Barnett, R. (1990) *The Idea of Higher Education* (Buckingham: Open University Press).

Basnett, S. (2004a) 'The first rung' in *How to Get Promoted: A Career Guide for Academics* (London: Times Higher Education Supplement), 8–11.

Basnett, S. (2004b) 'Ditch the smocks – dress to impress', *Times Higher Education Supplement*, 29 October, 54.

Blaxter, L., Hughes, C. and Tight, M. (1998) *The Academic Career Handbook* (Buckingham: Open University Press).

Brew, A. (2006) *Research and Teaching* (Basingstoke: Palgrave Macmillan).

Brown, S. and Race, P. (2002) *Lecturing: A Practical Guide* (London: Kogan Page).

Burnham, P. (1997a) 'Introduction' in P. Burnham (ed.) *Surviving the Research Process in Politics* (London: Pinter), 1–11.

Burnham, P. (1997b) 'Surviving the viva' in P. Burnham (ed.) *Surviving the Research Process* (London: Pinter), 193–9.

Burnham, P., Gilland, K., Grant, W. and Layton-Henry, Z. (2004) *Research Methods in Politics* (Basingstoke: Palgrave Macmillan).

Charkin, R. (2005) 'Evolving to thrive in a digital landscape', *Connected*, December, 2.

Deem, R. (2003a) 'Gender, organizational cultures and the practices of manager-academics in UK universities', *Gender, Work and Organization*, 10 (2), 239–59.

Deem, R. (2003b) 'Managing to exclude? Manager-academics and staff communities in contemporary UK universities', in M. Tight (ed.) *International Perspectives on Higher Education Research: Access and Inclusion* (Boston: Elsevier Science/JAI).

Delamont, S., Atkinson, P. and Parry, O. (1997) *Supervising the PhD: A Guide to Success* (Buckingham: Open University Press).

Dunleavy, P. (2003) *Authoring a PhD* (Basingstoke: Palgrave Macmillan).

Eadie, P. (2005) 'The rise of the teaching fellow: between a rock and a hardplace?' *BISA News*, November.

Edwards, H., Smith, G. and Webb, G. (eds) (2001) *Lecturing: Case Studies, Experience and Practice* (London: Kogan Page).

Entwistle, N. (1988) *Styles of Learning and Teaching* (London: David Fulton).

Evidence (2003) *Funding Research Diversity* (London: Universities UK).

Frean, A. (2004) 'Young, gifted, wrecked: high fliers brought low', *The Times*, 25 July, p. 28.

Gibbs, G. and Habeshaw, T. (1989) *Preparing to Teach: An Introduction to Effective Teaching in Higher Education* (Bristol: Technical and Educational Series).

Goldsmith, J., Komlos, J. and Gold, P. S. (2001) *The Chicago Guide to Your Academic Career* (Chicago: University of Chicago Press).

Gordon, G. (2005) 'The human dimensions of the research agenda: supporting the development of researchers throughout the career life cycle', *Higher Education Quarterly*, 59 (1), 40–55.

Gruss, P. (2005) 'Note from the president' in *Research Perspectives of the Max Planck Society* (Munich: Max Planck Society), 4–5.

Jackson, P. and Tinkler, P. (2004) 'Why we recommend greater openness for PhD vivas', *Times Higher Education Supplement*, 19 March, 14.

Jarvis, P., Holford, J., and Griffin, C. (2003) *The Theory and Practice of Learning*, 2nd edn (London: Kogan Page).

Jenkins, A., Breen, R. and Lindsay, R. (2003) *Reshaping Teaching in Higher Education: Linking Teaching with Research* (London: Kogan Page).

Kennedy, S. (2004) 'Cutting edge is decidedly blunt', *Times Higher Education Supplement*, 3 December.

Lewis, H. and Hills, P. (1999) *Time Management for Academics* (Dereham: Peter Francis).

Lucas, C. J. and Murry, J. W., Jnr. (2002) *New Faculty: A Practical Guide for Academic Beginners* (New York: Palgrave).

Luey, B. (2002) *Handbook for Academic Authors*, 4th edn (Cambridge: Cambridge University Press).

Maier, P. and Warren, A. (2000) *Integrating Technology in Learning and Teaching: A Practical Guide for Educators* (London: Kogan Page).

Massy, W. F. (2003) *Honoring the Trust: Quality and Cost Containment in Higher Education* (Bolton, Mass.: Arter).

Max Planck Society (2005) *Research Perspectives of the Max Planck Society* (Munich: Max Planck Society).

May, T. (2001) *Social Research*, 3rd edn (Maidenhead: Open University Press).

Middlehurst, R. (1995) *Leading Academics* (Buckingham: Open University Press).

Moran, M. (2005) 'The vanishing textbook', *Political Studies Association News*, 16 (2), 4.

Newman, J. H. (1982) *The Idea of a University* (London: University of Notre Dame Press).

Page, E. (1997) 'The second year and how to survive it' in P. Burnham (ed.) *Surviving the Research Process in Politics* (London: Pinter), 51–61.

Park, R. (2003) 'Levelling the playing field: towards best practice in the doctoral viva', *Higher Education Review*, 36 (1), 24–36.

Persaud, R. (2001) *Staying Sane* (London: Bantam).

Quality Assurance Agency (QAA) (2004) *Code of practice for the assurance of academic quality and standards in higher education, Section 1: Postgraduate research programmes* (Gloucester: Quality Assurance Agency for Higher Education).

Race, P. (2001) *The Lecturer's Toolkit: A Practical Guide to Learning, Teaching and Assessment*, 2nd edn (London: Kogan Page).

RAE (2004) *RAE 2008: Initial Decisions by the UK Funding Bodies* (Bristol: Higher Education Funding Council for England).

RAE (2005) *RAE 2008: Guidance to Panels* (Bristol: Higher Education Funding Council for England).

Robinson, N. (1997) 'The student–supervisor relationship' in P. Burnham (ed.) *Surviving the Research Process in Politics* (London: Pinter), 71–82.

Sanders, P. (2002) *First Steps in Counselling*, 3rd edn (Ross-on-Wye: PCCS).

Squires, G. (2003) *Trouble-shooting Your Teaching: A Step-by-step Guide to Analysing and Improving Your Practice* (London: Kogan Page).

Tinkler, P and Jackson, C. (2004) *The Doctoral Examination Process* (Maidenhead: Open University Press).

Tufte, E.R. (2003) *The Cognitive Style of PowerPoint* (Cheshire, Conn.: Graphics Press).

Tytherleigh, P. and Cooper, C. (2003) 'Lives on the rocks', *Times Higher Education Supplement*, 23 October.

Van der Berghe, P. (1970) *Academic Gamesmanship* (New York: Abelard-Schuman).

Index